The Merrill Studies
in
Walden

CHARLES E. MERRILL STUDIES
Under the General Editorship of
Matthew J. Bruccoli and Joseph Katz

The Merrill Studies
in
Walden

Compiled by

Joseph J. Moldenhauer
The University of Texas at Austin

Charles E. Merrill Publishing Company
A Bell & Howell Company
Columbus, Ohio

ISBN: 0-675-09193-4

Library of Congress Catalog Card Number: 75-153768

1 2 3 4 5 6 7 — 77 76 75 74 73 72 71

Printed in the United States of America

Preface

"I have lately added an absurdity or two to my usual ones," Ralph Waldo Emerson informed his brother William on October 4, 1844, and proceeded to describe his purchase of some rural real estate at an average cost of $15.29 per acre. By the acquisition he became "landlord & waterlord of 14 acres, more or less, on the shore of Walden & can raise my own blackberries." Berries the tract yielded, and beans, and books; Emerson could not foresee how rich a crop his field was to bear for Henry Thoreau, and through Thoreau for the world. Like the Walden waters that mingled with those of the Ganges, "Civil Disobedience," *A Week on the Concord and Merrimack Rivers*, and *Walden*, products of Thoreau's residence beside the pond, have entered into a commerce more truly universal than the ice-trade.

This collection of responses to *Walden* begins with a series of extracts from letters and journals (two of which antedate the publication of *Walden* in 1854 but interestingly anticipate more formal discussions) and three contemporary reviews. The notices by Lydia Child and George Eliot are warmly sympathetic; the *Knickerbocker* review, while less friendly, displays the high spirits characteristic of *Walden* itself and of much good *Walden* criticism. These and other early notices concentrate on Thoreau's ethical and economic challenge to his times. Between Thoreau's death in 1862 and the turn of the century, comment on *Walden* typically occurred in more general assessments of the author's personality and ideas. The essays reprinted in section 2 enlist and deploy the images of Thoreau which dominated criticism for half a century: the Stoic, the Skulker, the Naturalist, the Aphorist, the Spiritual Invalid, the Prophet, the Manly Thoreau, the Unmanly Thoreau, the Imitator of Emerson, the Natural Man, the Seeker after Noble Purity. My four selections comprise a lively if sometimes injudicious debate on the social worth of the man and (at least implicitly) the values and dangers of the book. I have reluctantly omitted, for want of space, Bronson Alcott's tribute, "The Forester," Bradford Torrey's "Thoreau," a selection from Henry Salt's biography, and George W. Cooke's "The Two Thoreaus," all of which the reader will find listed in Walter Harding's *A Thoreau Handbook* (1959).

Excepting Mark Van Doren's *Critical Study* of Thoreau, nothing of great consequence was written on *Walden* or its author between 1897 and the centennial of his birth in 1917. In the two decades following, however, Thoreau's writings were given a precise philosophical scrutiny which they had not yet received, and were studied

v

in their political and economic context by a generation of critics attuned to the social sciences. These tendencies are represented in section 3 by the Foerster and Canby pieces. Another epoch in Thoreau studies began with the publication of *American Renaissance* (1941) by F. O. Matthiessen, who related Thoreau's aesthetics to foreign and domestic Romanticisms and offered the first clear formulation of the deliberate artistry of *Walden*, its structure and texture as a literary entity. To Matthiessen's analysis most subsequent interpretations are in some degree beholden, and I reprint a substantial extract. The remainder of this gathering consists of mythic, symbolic, stylistic or rhetorical, thematic, and structural explorations of *Walden*, plus one more essay (Miller's) which examines it in terms of Romantic norms of taste. The difficulty of isolating sections which focus on *Walden* or the narrow confines of this anthology have prevented my including part of Van Doren's book, Archibald MacMechan's vigorous chapter in the *C.H.A.L.*, Gilbert Seldes' "Thoreau," Max Lerner's "Thoreau: No Hermit," a biologist's appraisal of *Walden* by Edward S. Deevey, Jr., Stanley Edgar Hyman's fine "Henry Thoreau in Our Time," Raymond Adams' inquiry into Thoreau's mock-heroics, Leo Stoller's "Thoreau's Doctrine of Simplicity," an excerpt from J. Lyndon Shanley's genetic study, *The Making of Walden*, Bruce King's "Thoreau's *Walden*," John B. Pickard's "The Religion of 'Higher Laws,'" and a portion of Edwin Fussell's *Frontier: American Literature and the American West*. Together with the omitted materials I mentioned earlier, these would form a collection as large as the present volume. I recommend them highly, and confess that my delight in reviewing the whole body of responses to *Walden*—testimony to its perennial power of stimulation—was almost offset by my frustration when choices had to be made.

I have attempted, however, to provide a balanced historical collection, representing the major directions of *Walden* pondering in essays distinguished by their perceptiveness, inventiveness, and influence. Accordingly, I have arranged the essays in chronological order, and from several I have deleted passages which seemed relatively inapplicable to *Walden*, marking the omissions with ellipses.

J. M.

Contents

3. Twentieth-Century Readings

1. Contemporary Letters, Journals and Reviews

Letters and Journals

As for Thoreau, there is one chance in a thousand that he might write a most excellent and readable book; but I should be sorry to take the responsibility, either towards you or him, of stirring him up to write anything . . . He is the most unmalleable fellow alive—the most tedious, tiresome, and intolerable—the narrowest and most notional—and yet, true as all this is, he has great qualities of intellect and character. The only way, however, in which he could ever approach the popular mind, would be by writing a book of simple observation of nature, somewhat in the vein of White's *History of Selborne*.

Nathaniel Hawthorne to Evert Duyckinck, 1845; in F. O. Matthiessen, *American Renaissance* (New York: Oxford University Press, 1941), p. 196.

. . . Henry . . . is preparing his Book for the press and the title is to be, Waldien (I dont know how to spell it) or life in the Woods. I think the title will take if the Book dont. I was quite amused with what Sophia told me her mother said about it the other day, she poor girl was lying in bed with a sick head ache when she heard Cynthia (who has grown rather nervous of late) telling over her troubles to Mrs. Dunbar, after speaking of her own and Helen's sickness, she says . . . Henry is putting things into his Book that never ought to be there . . . As for Henry's book, you know I have said, there were parts of it that sounded to me very much like blasphemy, and I did not believe they would publish it, on reading it to Helen the other day Sophia told me, she made the same remark, and coming from her, Henry was much surprised, and said she did not understand it, but still I fear they will not persuade him to leave it out.

Maria Thoreau to Prudence Ward, February 28, 1849; in Henry Seidel Canby, *Thoreau* (Boston: Houghton Mifflin Company, 1939), pp. 248–49. Reprinted by permission of the publisher.

"Walden" published. Elder-berries. Waxwork yellowing.

Thoreau, journal entry for August 9, 1854; *The Writings of Henry David Thoreau* (Boston: Houghton Mifflin Company, 1906), XII, 429.

I have just finished reading "Walden" and hasten to thank you for the great degree of satisfaction it has afforded me. Having always been a lover of Nature, in man, as well as in the material universe, I hail with pleasure every original production in literature which bears the stamp of a genuine and earnest love for the true philosophy of human life.—Such I assure you I esteem your book to be. To many, and to most, it will appear to be the wild musings of an eccentric and strange mind, though all must recognize your affectionate regard for the gentle denizens of the woods and pond as well as the great love you have shewn for what are familiarly called the beauties of Nature. But to me the book appears to evince a mind most thoroughly self possessed, highly cultivated with a strong vein of common sense. The whole book is a prose poem (pardon the solecism) and at the same time as simple as a running brook.

Daniel Ricketson to Thoreau, August 12,
1854; in *The Correspondence of Henry David Thoreau,*
ed. Walter Harding and Carl Bode (New York: New
York University Press, 1958), p. 332.

Let me thank you heartily for your paper on the present condition of Massachusetts, read at Framingham and printed in the *Liberator.* As a literary statement of the truth, which every day is making more manifest, it surpasses everything else (so I think), which the terrible week in Boston has called out. I need hardly add my thanks for "Walden," which I have been awaiting for so many years. Through Mr. Field's kindness, I have read a great deal of it in sheets:—I have just secured two copies, one for myself, and one for a young girl here, who seems to me to have the most remarkable literary talent since Margaret Fuller,—and to whom your first book has been among the scriptures, ever since I gave her that. No doubt your new book will have a larger circulation than the other, but not, I think, a more select or appreciate one.

Thomas Wentworth Higginson to Thoreau,
August 13, 1854; in *The Correspondence,* p. 336.

All American kind are delighted with "Walden" as far as they have dared say[.] The little pond sinks in these very days as tremulous at its human fame. I do not know if the book has come to you yet;—but it is cheerful, sparkling, readable, with all kinds of merits, & rising sometimes to very great heights. We account Henry the undoubted King of all American lions. He is walking up & down Concord, firm-looking, but in a tremble of great expectation.

> Ralph Waldo Emerson to George Partridge Bradford, August 28, 1854; in *The Letters of Ralph Waldo Emerson*, ed. Ralph L. Rusk (New York: Columbia University Press, 1939), IV, 459–60.

R. W. E. told [of] Mr. Hill, his classmate, of Bangor, who was much interested in my "Walden," but relished it merely as a capital satire and joke, and even thought that the survey and map of the pond were not real, but a caricature of the Coast Surveys.

> Thoreau, journal entry for January 5, 1855; *Writings*, XIII, 102–3.

I forwarded to you by mail on the 31st of January a copy of my "Week," post paid, which I trust that you have received. I thank you heartily for the expression of your interest in "Walden" and hope that you will not be disappointed by the "Week." You ask how the former has been received. It has found an audience of excellent character, and quite numerous, some 2000 copies having been dispersed. I should consider it a greater success to interest one wise and earnest soul, than a million unwise & frivolous.

You may rely on it that you have the best of me in my books, and that I am not worth seeing personally—the stuttering, blundering, clod-hopper that I am. Even poetry, you know, is in one sense an infinite brag & exaggeration. Not that I do not stand on all that I have written—but what am I to the truth I feebly utter!

> Thoreau to Calvin Greene, February 10, 1856; in *The Correspondence*, p. 407.

Lydia Maria Child [*?*]

[Review of *A Week on the Concord and Merrimack Rivers* and *Walden*]

These books spring from a depth of thought which will not suffer them to be put by, and are written in a spirit in striking contrast with that which is uppermost in our time and country. Out of the heart of practical, hard-working, progressive New England come these Oriental utterances. The life exhibited in them teaches us, much more impressively than any number of sermons could, that this Western activity of which we are so proud, these material improvements, this commercial enterprise, this rapid accumulation of wealth, even our external, associated philanthropic action, are very easily overrated. The true glory of the human soul is not to be reached by the most rapid travelling in car or steamboat, by the instant transmission of intelligence however far, by the most speedy accumulation of a fortune, and however efficient measures we may adopt for the reform of the intemperate, the emancipation of the enslaved, &c., it will avail little unless we are ourselves essentially noble enough to inspire those whom we would so benefit with nobleness. External bondage is trifling compared with the bondage of an ignoble soul. Such things are often said, doubtless, in pulpits and elsewhere, but the men who say them are too apt to live just with the crowd, and so their words come more and more to ring with a hollow sound.

It is refreshing to find in these books the sentiments of one man whose aim manifestly is to *live*, and not to waste his time upon the externals of living. Educated at Cambridge, in the way called liberal, he seems determined to make a liberal life of it, and not to become the slave of any calling, for the sake of earning a reputable livelihood or of being regarded as a useful member of society. He evidently considers it his first business to become more and more a living, advancing soul, knowing that thus alone (though he desires to think as little as possible about that) can he be, in any proper sense, useful to others. Mr. Thoreau's view of life has been called selfish. His own words, under the head of "Philanthropy" in Wal-

---

Reprinted from the *National Anti-Slavery Standard,* 16 December 1854, p. 3.

den, are the amplest defense against this charge, to those who can appreciate them. In a deeper sense than we commonly think, charity begins at home. The man who, with any fidelity, obeys his own genius, serves men infinitely more by so doing, becoming an encouragement, a strengthener, a fountain of inspiration to them, than if he were to turn aside from his path and exhaust his energies in striving to meet their superficial needs. As a thing by the way, aside from our proper work, we may seek to remove external obstacles from the path of our neighbours, but no man can help them much who makes that his main business, instead of seeking evermore, with all his energies, to reach the loftiest point which his imagination sets before him, thus adding to the stock of true nobleness in the world.

But suppose all men should pursue Mr. Thoreau's course, it is asked triumphantly, as though, then, we should be sure to go back to barbarism. Let it be considered, in the first place, that no man could pursue his course who was a mere superficial imitator, any more than it would be a real imitation of Christ if all men were to make it their main business to go about preaching the Gospel to each other. Is it progress toward barbarism to simplify one's outward life for the sake of coming closer to Nature and to the realm of ideas? Is it civilization and refinement to be occupied evermore with adding to our material conveniences, comforts and luxuries, to make ourselves not so much living members as dead tools of society, in some bank, shop, office, pulpit or kitchen? If men were to follow in Mr. Thoreau's steps, by being more obedient to their loftiest instincts, there would, indeed, be a falling off in the splendor of our houses, in the richness of our furniture and dress, in the luxury of our tables, but how poor are these things in comparison with the new grandeur and beauty which would appear in the souls of men. What fresh and inspiring conversation should we have, instead of the wearisome gossip, which now meets us at every turn. Men toil on, wearing out body or soul, or both, that they may accumulate a needless amount of the externals of living; that they may win the regard of those no wiser than themselves; their natures become warped and hardened to their pursuits; they get fainter and fainter glimpses of the glory of the world, and, by and by, comes into their richly-adorned parlours some wise and beautiful soul, like the writer of these books, who, speaking from the fullness of his inward life, makes their luxuries appear vulgar, showing that, in a direct way, he has obtained the essence of that which his entertainers have been vainly seeking for at such a terrible expense.

It seems remarkable that these books have received no more adequate notice in our Literary Journals. But the class of scholars are often as blind as others to any new elevation of soul. In Putnam's Magazine, Mr. Thoreau is spoken of as an oddity, as the Yankee Diogenes, as though the really ridiculous oddity were not in us of the "starched shirt-collar" rather than in this devotee of Nature and Thought. Some have praised the originality and profound sympathy with which he views natural objects. We might as well stop with praising Jesus for the happy use he has made of the lilies of the field. The fact of surpassing interest for us is the simple grandeur of Mr. Thoreau's position—a position open to us all, and of which this sympathy with Nature is but a single result. This is seen in the less descriptive, more purely thoughtful passages, such as that upon Friendship in the "Wednesday" of the "Week," and in those upon "Solitude," "What I Lived for," and "Higher Laws," in "Walden," as well as in many others in both books. We do not believe that, in the whole course of literature, ancient and modern, so noble a discourse upon Friendship can be produced as that which Mr. Thoreau has given us. It points to a relation, to be sure, which, from the ordinary level of our lives, may seem remote and dreamy. But it is our thirst for, and glimpses of, such things which indicate the greatness of our nature, which give the purest charm and colouring to our lives. The striking peculiarity of Mr. Thoreau's attitude is, that while he is no religionist, and while he is eminently practical in regard to the material economics of life, he yet manifestly feels, through and through, that the loftiest dreams of the imagination are the solidest realities, and so the only foundation for us to build upon, while the affairs in which men are everywhere busying themselves so intensely are comparatively the merest froth and foam.

Town and Rural Humbugs

When Philip, King of Macedon, had made preparations to march against the Corinthians, the latter, though utterly incapable of coping with that sagacious and powerful monarch, affected to make great efforts at defence with a view to resist him. Diogenes, who took great delight in ridiculing such follies as he was too proud to indulge in himself, or did not happen to have a taste for, began to roll about his tub in a bustling and excited manner, thus deriding the idle hurry and silly show of opposition by which the feeble Corinthians were trying to deceive themselves or Philip into a belief that he had something to fear from them.

It is a wonder to a certain Yankee Diogenes, that there are not more tubs rolled about now-a-days; for the world, in his estimation, never contained more bustling, shadow-pursuing Corinthians, than at the present time.

A Concord philosopher, or modern Diogenes, who has an eye of acute penetration in looking out upon the world, discovered so much aimless and foolish bustle, such a disproportion of shams to realities, that his inclination or self-respect would not permit him to participate in them; so he built himself in the woods, on the banks of a pond of pure water—deep enough for drowning purposes if the bean-crop failed—a tub of unambitious proportions, into which he crawled. In this retreat, where he supported animal and intellectual life for more than two years, at a cost of about thirteen (!) dollars per annum, he wrote a book full of interest, containing the most pithy, sharp, and original remarks.

It is a fortunate circumstance for Mr. Thoreau, the name of this eccentric person, that his low estimate of the value of the objects, compared with their cost, for which the world is so assiduously and painfully laboring, should have received, so soon after the publication of his book, such an important, substantial, and practical confirmation in the auto-biography of Barnum. If any thing is calculated to induce a man to see how few beans will support animal life, we think it is a contemplation of the life and career of the great show-man. If there is any thing calculated to reconcile us, not to the career of Barnum, but to whatever laborious drudgery may be

Reprinted from *The Knickerbocker,* XLV (March 1855), 235–41.

necessary to procure good beef-steaks and oysters, with their necessary accompaniments, it is the thought of those inevitable beans, that constituted so large a part of the *crop* of Mr. Thoreau, and that extraordinary compound of corn-meal and water, which he facetiously called bread.

Beyond all question, the two most remarkable books that have been published the last year are the 'Auto-biography of Barnum,' and 'Life in the Woods,' by Thoreau. The authors of the two books, in tastes, habits, disposition, and culture are perfect antipodes to each other; and the lessons they inculcate are consequently diametrically opposite. If ever a book required an antidote, it is the auto-biography of Barnum, and we know of no other so well calculated to furnish this antidote as the book of Thoreau's.

If any of the readers of the KNICKERBOCKER have so long denied themselves the pleasure of reading 'Walden, or Life in the Woods,' we will give them a slight account of the book and its author; but we presume the information will be necessary to only very few. Mr. Thoreau is a graduate of Harvard University. He is a bold and original thinker; 'he reads much, is a great observer, and looks quite through the deeds of men.' 'Beware,' says Emerson, 'when the great GOD lets loose a thinker on this planet. Then all things are at risk.' Are thinkers so rare that all the moral, social, and political elements of society may be disturbed by the advent of one? The sale Barnum's book has already met with is not, to be sure, suggestive of an overwhelming number of thinkers in the country. Thinkers always have been considered dangerous. Even Caesar, if he could have feared any thing, would have been afraid of that lean Cassius, because

'He thinks too much: such men are dangerous.'

And why are thinkers dangerous? Because the world is full of 'time-honored and venerable' shams, which the words of thinkers are apt to endanger.

After leaving college, Mr. Thoreau doffed the harness which society enjoins that all its members shall wear, in order for them 'to get along well,' but it galled and chafed in so many places that he threw it off, and took to the woods in Concord. He built a hut there, a mile from any neighbors, that cost him twenty-eight dollars, twelve and a-half cents, and lived there more than two years— eight months of the time at an expense of nearly nine shillings a-month. Before adopting this mode of life, he first tried school-

keeping, reporting for a newspaper, and then trading for a livelihood; but after a short trial at each, became persuaded that it was
impossible for his genius to lie in either of those channels.

After hesitating for some time as to the advisability of seeking
a living by picking huckle-berries, he at last concluded that 'the
occupation of a day-laborer was the most independent of any, as
it required only thirty or forty days in a year to support one. The
laborer's day ends with the going down of the sun, and he is then
free to devote himself to his chosen pursuit, independent of his
labor; but his employer, who speculates from month to month, has
no respite from one end of the year to the other. In short, I am
convinced, both by faith and experience, that to maintain one's self
on this earth, is not a hardship, but a pastime, if we will live simply
and wisely, as the pursuits of the simpler nations are still the sports
of the more artificial. It is not necessary that a man should earn his
living by the sweat of his brow, unless he sweats easier than I do.'

The establishment in the woods, kept up by the extravagant
expenditures we have mentioned before, was the result of these
reflections.

If there is any reader of the KNICKERBOCKER—native-born and
a Know-Nothing—who needs to be told who P. T. BARNUM is, such
a person might, without doubt, 'hear something to his advantage,'
by inquiring out and presenting himself before that illustrious individual; for the great show-man has made a good deal of money by
exhibiting less extraordinary animals than such a man would be.

It was pretty well understood by physiologists, before the recent
experiment of Mr. Thoreau, how little farinaceous food would suffice for the human stomach; and Chatham-street clothiers have a
tolerably accurate knowledge of how little poor and cheap raiment
will suffice to cover the back, so that his 'life in the woods' adds
but little to the stock of information scientific men already possessed. But it was not clearly known to what extent the public
was gullible until the auto-biography of Barnum fully demonstrated
the fact. This renowned individual has shown to a dignified and
appreciative public the vulgar machinery used to humbug them,
and they (the public) are convulsed with laughter and delight at
the exposition. 'Cuteness is held in such great esteem that the fact
of being egregiously cajoled and fooled out of our money is lost
sight of in admiration for the shrewdness of the man who can do it.
And then there is such an idolatrous worship of the almighty dollar,
that the man who accumulates 'a pile' is pretty sure to have the
laugh on his side. 'Let him laugh who wins,' says Barnum, and the

whole country says amen. It is very evident that shams sometimes 'pay better' pecuniarily than realities, but we doubt if they
do in all respects. Although Thoreau 'realized' from his bean-crop
one season—a summer's labor—but eight dollars seventy-one and
a-half cents, yet it is painful to think what Barnum must have
'realized' from 'Joice Heth' and the 'Woolly Horse.'

If we were obliged to choose between being shut up in 'conven-
tionalism's air-tight stove,' (even if the said stove had all the surroundings of elegance and comforts that wealth could buy,) and
a twenty-eight dollar tub in the woods, with a boundless range of
freedom in the daily *walks* of life, we should not hesitate a moment
in taking the tub, if it were not for a recollection of those horrid
beans, and that melancholy mixture of meal and water. Aye, there's
the rub; for from that vegetable diet what dreams might come,
when we had shuffled off the wherewith to purchase other food,
must give us pause. There's the consideration that makes the sorry
conventionalisms of society of so long life. We rather bear those
ills we have, than fly to others that we know not of. A very reasonable dread of something unpleasant resulting to us from eating
beans in great quantities, would be likely to be a consequence of
our experience alone, if we happened to be deficient in physiological
knowledge. Whatever effects, however, different kinds of diet may
have upon different persons, mentally or physically, nothing is more
clear than the fact that the diet of Mr. Thoreau did not make him
mentally windy. We think, however, between Iranistan, with Joice
Heth and the Mermaid for associates, and the tub at Walden, with
only Shakespeare for a companion, few probably would be long
puzzled in making a choice, though we are constrained to say that
the great majority would undoubtedly be on the side of the natural
phenomena—we mean on the side of Barnum and the other mentioned curiosities. Still, in contemplating a good many of the situations in which Barnum was placed, it is impossible to conceive that
any person of a comparatively sensitive nature would not gladly
have exchanged places with the man of the woods. (We refer of
course to the author of 'Walden,' and not to the animal known as
'the man of the woods.' Some perhaps would not have taken pains
to make this explanation.)

There is a good deal more virtue in beans than we supposed there
was, if they are sufficient to sustain a man in such cheerful spirits
as Thoreau appears to have been in when he wrote that book. The
spirit oftentimes may be strong when the flesh is weak; but there
does not appear to be any evidence of weakness of the flesh in the

author of 'Walden.' We cannot help feeling admiration for the man

> 'THAT fortune's buffets and rewards
> Hast ta'en with equal thanks:'

and since Sylla so coolly massacred so many Roman citizens, there
has not been a man who apparently has contemplated his fellow-
men with a more cheerful, lofty, and philosophical scorn than the
occupant of this Walden tub. If a man can do this upon beans, or
in *spite* of them, we shall endeavor to cultivate a respect for that
vegetable, which we never could endure.

It was a philosopher, as ancient as Aristotle, we believe, who
affirmed that 'they most resemble the gods whose wants were few-
est.' Whether the sentiment is a true one or not, we have no hesita-
tion in saying that the gods we worship will bear a good deal more
resemblance to H. D. Thoreau than to P. T. Barnum. We believe
it requires a much higher order of intellect to live alone in the
woods, than to dance attendance in the museum of a great metrop-
olis upon dead hyenas and boa constrictors, living monkeys and
rattle-snakes, giants and dwarfs, artificial mermaids, and natural
zanies. There is, however, a good deal of society worse than this.

Of the many good things said by Colton, one of the best, we
think, is the following:

> 'Expense of thought is the rarest prodigality, and to dare to live
> alone the rarest courage; since there are many who had rather
> meet their bitterest enemy in the field, than their own hearts in
> their closet. He that has no resources of mind is more to be pitied
> than he who is in want of necessaries for the body; and to be
> obliged to beg our daily happiness from others, bespeaks a more
> lamentable poverty than that of him who begs his daily bread.'

We do not believe there is any danger of proselytes to Mr.
Thoreau's mode of life becoming too numerous. We wish we could
say the same in regard to Barnum's. We ask the reader to look
around among his acquaintances, and see if the number of those
whose resources of mind are sufficient to enable them to dispense
with much intercourse with others, is not exceedingly small. We
know of some such, though they are very few; but their fondness
for solitude unfortunately is not associated with any particular admiration for a vegetable diet. It is a melancholy circumstance, and
one that has been very bitterly deplored, ever since that indefinite

period when 'the memory of man runneth not to the contrary,' that the accompaniments of poverty should go hand-in-hand with a taste for a solitary life. A hearty appreciation of and love for humble fare, plain clothes, and poor surroundings generally, are what men of genius need to cultivate. 'Walden' tends to encourage this cultivation.

The part of Mr. Barnum's life, during which he has become a millionaire, has been spent almost wholly in a crowd. It would be no paradox to say that if the time he has spent as a show-man had been spent in the woods, neither the brilliancy of his imagination nor the vigor and originality of his thoughts would have enabled him to have produced a book that would have created any very great excitement, notwithstanding the extraordinary attributes of that intellect which could conceive the idea of combining nature and art to produce 'natural curiosities,' and which was shrewd enough to contrive ways and means for drawing quarters and shillings, and for the smallest value received, indiscriminately from residents in the Fifth Avenue and the Five-Points, from the statesman and 'the Bowery-boy,' from savans, theologians, lawyers, doctors, merchants, and 'the rest of mankind,' to say nothing about Queen Victoria, the Duke of Wellington, and a large portion of the Eastern continent beside.

Unlike as Barnum and Thoreau are in most every other respect, in one point there is a striking resemblance. Both of them had no idea of laboring very hard with their hands for a living; they were determined to support themselves principally by their wits. The genius of Barnum led him to obtain the meat he fed upon by a skillful combination of nature with art—by eking out the shortcomings in the animal creation with ingenious and elaborate manufactures, and then adroitly bringing the singular compounds thus formed to bear upon the credulity of the public. And thus, while he taxed the animal, vegetable, and mineral kingdoms, either separately or combined, to gratify the curiosity of the public, the most valued products of the last-mentioned kingdom flowered in a large and perpetual stream into his pocket. But his expenditures of 'brass' in these labors were enormous. Thoreau had no talent for 'great combinations.' The meat he fed upon evidently would not be that of extraordinary calves or over-grown buffaloes, baked in the paragon cooking-stove of public curiosity; or rather, as he ate no meat, the vegetables he lived upon would not come from the exhibition of India-rubber mermaids, gutta-percha fish, or mammoth squashes. His genius did not lie at all in that direction. On the contrary, he preferred to diminish his wants, instead of resorting to extraordinary schemes to gratify them. . . .

We said some little way back that there was one point of resemblance between Barnum and Thoreau. There are half-a-dozen. Both are good-natured, genial, pleasant men. One sneers at and ridicules the pursuits of his contemporaries with the same cheerfulness and good-will that the other cajoles and fleeces them. The rural philosopher measured the length, breadth, and depth of Walden Pond, with the same jovial contentedness that the metropolitan show-man measured the length, breadth, and depth of the public gullibility. Both too are compassionate men. Flashes of pity are occasionally met with in the book of Barnum's, at the extent of the credulity of that public he seemingly so remorselessly wheedled; and Thoreau evinced a good deal of compassion for some of his well-to-do townsmen. His sympathy was a good deal moved in behalf of the farmer that owned 'a handsome property,' who was driving his oxen in the night to Brighton, through the mud and darkness. Both were artists. He of the wood constructed himself the unpretending edifice he occupied—a representation of which graces the title-page of his book. Barnum's artistic skill was more evinced in constructing such 'curiosities' as we have before alluded to. And finally, both were humbugs—one a town and the other a rural humbug.

But both of them have nevertheless made large contributions to the science of human nature. Malherbe, once upon hearing a prose work of great merit extolled, dryly asked if it would *reduce the price of bread!* If 'Walden' should be extensively read, we think it would have the effect to reduce somewhat the price of meat, if it did not of bread. At all events it encourages the belief, which in this utilitarian age enough needs encouragement, that there is some other object to live for except 'to make money.'

In the New-England philosophy of life, which so extensively prevails where the moral or intellectual character of a man is more or less determined by his habits of *thrift*, such a book as 'Walden' was needed. Extravagant as it is in the notions it promulgates, we think it is nevertheless calculated to do a good deal of good, and we hope it will be widely read. Where it exerts a bad influence upon one person, Barnum's auto-biography will upon a hundred.

[Review of *Walden*]

... in a volume called "Walden; or, Life in the Woods"—published last year, but quite interesting enough to make it worth while for us to break our rule by a retrospective notice—we have a bit of pure American life (not the "go a-head" species, but its opposite pole), animated by that energetic, yet calm spirit of innovation, that practical as well as theoretic independence of formulæ, which is peculiar to some of the finer American minds. The writer tells us how he chose, for some years, to be a stoic of the woods; how he built his house; how he earned the necessaries of his simple life by cultivating a bit of ground. He tells his system of diet, his studies, his reflections, and his observations of natural phenomena. These last are not only made by a keen eye, but have their interest enhanced by passing through the medium of a deep poetic sensibility; and, indeed, we feel throughout the book the presence of a refined as well as a hardy mind. People—very wise in their own eyes—who would have every man's life ordered according to a particular pattern, and who are intolerant of every existence the utility of which is not palpable to them, may pooh-pooh Mr. Thoreau and this episode in his history, as unpractical and dreamy. Instead of contesting their opinion ourselves, we will let Mr. Thoreau speak for himself. There is plenty of sturdy sense mingled with his unworldliness. . . .

Reprinted from *Westminster Review*, LXV (January 1856), 302–3.

2. Appreciations and Disparagements

Thoreau

. . . At this time, a strong, healthy youth, fresh from college, whilst all his companions were choosing their profession, or eager to begin some lucrative employment, it was inevitable that his thoughts should be exercised on the same question, and it required rare decision to refuse all the accustomed paths, and keep his solitary freedom at the cost of disappointing the natural expectations of his family and friends: all the more difficult that he had a perfect probity, was exact in securing his own independence, and in holding every man to the like duty. But Thoreau never faltered. He was a born protestant. He declined to give up his large ambition of knowledge and action for any narrow craft or profession, aiming at a much more comprehensive calling, the art of living well. If he slighted and defied the opinions of others, it was only that he was more intent to reconcile his practice with his own belief. Never idle or self-indulgent, he preferred, when he wanted money, earning it by some piece of manual labor agreeable to him, as building a boat or a fence, planting, grafting, surveying, or other short work, to any long engagements. With his hardy habits and few wants, his skill in wood-craft, and his powerful arithmetic, he was very competent to live in any part of the world. It would cost him less time to supply his wants than another. He was therefore secure of his leisure.

A natural skill for mensuration, growing out of his mathematical knowledge, and his habit of ascertaining the measures and distances of objects which interested him, the size of trees, the depth and extent of ponds and rivers, the height of mountains, and the airline distance of his favorite summits,—this, and his intimate knowledge of the territory about Concord, made him drift into the profession of land-surveyor. It had the advantage for him that it led him continually into new and secluded grounds, and helped his studies of Nature. His accuracy and skill in this work were readily appreciated, and he found all the employment he wanted.

He could easily solve the problems of the surveyor, but he was daily beset with graver questions, which he manfully confronted. He interrogated every custom, and wished to settle all his practice on an ideal foundation. He was a protestant *à l'outrance*, and few

Reprinted from *Atlantic Monthly*, X (August 1862), 239–49.

lives contain so many renunciations. He was bred to no profession;
he never married; he lived alone; he never went to church; he never
voted; he refused to pay a tax to the State; he ate no flesh, he
drank no wine, he never knew the use of tobacco; and, though a
naturalist, he used neither trap nor gun. He chose, wisely, no doubt,
for himself, to be the bachelor of thought and Nature. He had no
talent for wealth, and knew how to be poor without the least hint
of squalor or inelegance. Perhaps he fell into his way of living without forecasting it much, but approved it with later wisdom. "I am
often reminded," he wrote in his journal, "that, if I had bestowed
on me the wealth of Crœsus, my aims must be still the same, and
my means essentially the same." He had no temptations to fight
against,—no appetites, no passions, no taste for elegant trifles. A
fine house, dress, the manners and talk of highly cultivated people
were all thrown away on him. He much preferred a good Indian,
and considered these refinements as impediments to conversation,
wishing to meet his companion on the simplest terms. He declined
invitations to dinner-parties, because there each was in every one's
way, and he could not meet the individuals to any purpose. "They
make their pride," he said, "in making their dinner cost much; I
make my pride in making my dinner cost little." When asked at
table what dish he preferred, he answered, "The nearest." He did
not like the taste of wine, and never had a vice in his life. He said,
—"I have a faint recollection of pleasure derived from smoking
dried lily-stems, before I was a man. I had commonly a supply of
these. I have never smoked anything more noxious."

He chose to be rich by making his wants few, and supplying
them himself. In his travels, he used the railroad only to get over
so much country as was unimportant to the present purpose, walking hundreds of miles, avoiding taverns, buying a lodging in farm-
ers' and fishermen's houses, as cheaper, and more agreeable to him,
and because there he could better find the men and the information he wanted.

There was somewhat military in his nature not to be subdued,
always manly and able, but rarely tender, as if he did not feel himself except in opposition. He wanted a fallacy to expose, a blunder
to pillory, I may say required a little sense of victory, a roll of the
drum, to call his powers into full exercise. It cost him nothing to
say No; indeed, he found it much easier than to say Yes. It seemed
as if his first instinct on hearing a proposition was to controvert it,
so impatient was he of the limitations of our daily thought. This
habit, of course, is a little chilling to the social affections; and

though the companion would in the end acquit him of any malice or untruth, yet it mars conversation. Hence, no equal companion stood in affectionate relations with one so pure and guileless. "I love Henry," said one of his friends, "but I cannot like him; and as for taking his arm, I should as soon think of taking the arm of an elm-tree.". . .

He was a speaker and actor of the truth,—born such,—and was ever running into dramatic situations from this cause. In any circumstance, it interested all bystanders to know what part Henry would take, and what he would say; and he did not disappoint expectation, but used an original judgment on each emergency. In 1845 he built himself a small framed house on the shores of Walden Pond, and lived there two years alone, a life of labor and study. This action was quite native and fit for him. No one who knew him would tax him with affectation. He was more unlike his neighbors in his thought than in his action. As soon as he had exhausted the advantages of that solitude, he abandoned it. In 1847, not approving some uses to which the public expenditure was applied, he refused to pay his town tax, and was put in jail. A friend paid the tax for him, and he was released. The like annoyance was threatened the next year. But, as his friends paid the tax, notwithstanding his protest, I believe he ceased to resist. No opposition or ridicule had any weight with him. He coldly and fully stated his opinion without affecting to believe that it was the opinion of the company. It was of no consequence, if every one present held the opposite opinion. . . .

Thoreau was sincerity itself, and might fortify the convictions of prophets in the ethical laws by his holy living. It was an affirmative experience which refused to be set aside. A truth-speaker he, capable of the most deep and strict conversation; a physician to the wounds of any soul; a friend, knowing not only the secret of friendship, but almost worshipped by those few persons who resorted to him as their confessor and prophet, and knew the deep value of his mind and great heart. He thought that without religion or devotion of some kind nothing great was ever accomplished: and he thought that the bigoted sectarian had better bear this in mind.

His virtues, of course, sometimes ran into extremes. It was easy to trace to the inexorable demand on all for exact truth that austerity which made this willing hermit more solitary even than he wished. Himself of a perfect probity, he required not less of others. He had a disgust at crime, and no worldly success would cover it.

He detected paltering as readily in dignified and prosperous persons as in beggars, and with equal scorn. Such dangerous frankness was in his dealing that his admirers called him "that terrible Thoreau," as if he spoke when silent, and was still present when he had departed. I think the severity of his ideal interfered to deprive him of a healthy sufficiency of human society.

The habit of a realist to find things the reverse of their appearance inclined him to put every statement in a paradox. A certain habit of antagonism defaced his earlier writings,—a trick of rhetoric not quite outgrown in his later, of substituting for the obvious word and thought its diametrical opposite. He praised wild mountains and winter forests for their domestic air, in snow and ice he would find sultriness, and commended the wilderness for resembling Rome and Paris. "It was so dry, that you might call it wet."

The tendency to magnify the moment, to read all the laws of Nature in the one object or one combination under your eye, is of course comic to those who do not share the philosopher's perception of identity. To him there was no such thing as size. The pond was a small ocean; the Atlantic, a large Walden Pond. He referred every minute fact to cosmical laws. Though he meant to be just, he seemed haunted by a certain chronic assumption that the science of the day pretended completeness, and he had just found out that the *savans* had neglected to discriminate a particular botanical variety, had failed to describe the seeds or count the sepals. "That is to say," we replied, "the blockheads were not born in Concord; but who said they were? It was their unspeakable misfortune to be born in London, or Paris, or Rome; but, poor fellows, they did what they could, considering that they never saw Bateman's Pond, or Nine-Acre Corner, or Becky-Stow's Swamp. Besides, what were you sent into the world for, but to add this observation?"

Had his genius been only contemplative, he had been fitted to his life, but with his energy and practical ability he seemed born for great enterprise and for command; and I so much regret the loss of his rare powers of action, that I cannot help counting it a fault in him that he had no ambition. Wanting this, instead of engineering for all America, he was the captain of a huckleberry-party. Pounding beans is good to the end of pounding empires one of these days; but if, at the end of years, it is still only beans!

But these foibles, real or apparent, were fast vanishing in the incessant growth of a spirit so robust and wise, and which effaced its defeats with new triumphs. His study of Nature was a perpetual ornament to him, and inspired his friends with curiosity to see the world through his eyes, and to hear his adventures. They possessed every kind of interest. . . .

James Russell Lowell

Thoreau

. . . Among the pistillate plants kindled to fruitage by the Emersonian pollen, Thoreau is thus far the most remarkable; and it is something eminently fitting that his posthumous works should be offered us by Emerson, for they are strawberries from his own garden. A singular mixture of varieties, indeed, there is;—alpine, some of them, with the flavor of rare mountain air; others wood, tasting of sunny roadside banks or shy openings in the forest; and not a few seedlings swollen hugely by culture, but lacking the fine natural aroma of the more modest kinds. Strange books these are of his, and interesting in many ways,—instructive chiefly as showing how considerable a crop may be raised on a comparatively narrow close of mind, and how much a man may make of his life if he will assiduously follow it, though perhaps never truly finding it at last.

We have just been renewing our recollection of Mr. Thoreau's writings, and have read through his six volumes in the order of their production. We shall try to give an adequate report of their impression upon us both as critic and as mere reader. He seems to us to have been a man with so high a conceit of himself that he accepted without questioning, and insisted on our accepting, his defects and weaknesses of character as virtues and powers peculiar to himself. Was he indolent, he finds none of the activities which attract or employ the rest of mankind worthy of him. Was he wanting in the qualities that make success, it is success that is contemptible, and not himself that lacks persistency and purpose.

Reprinted from a review of Thoreau's *Letters to Various Persons, North American Review,* CI (October 1865), 597–608. Lowell gave the essay its present title when reprinting it in *My Study Windows* (1871).

Was he poor, money was an unmixed evil. Did his life seem a selfish one, he condemns doing good as one of the weakest of superstitions. To be of use was with him the most killing bait of the wily tempter Uselessness. He had no faculty of generalization from outside of himself, or at least no experience which would supply the material of such, and he makes his own whim the law, his own range the horizon of the universe. He condemns a world, the hollowness of whose satisfactions he had never had the means of testing, and we recognize Apemantus behind the mask of Timon. He had little active imagination; of the receptive he had much. His appreciation is of the highest quality; his critical power, from want of continuity of mind, very limited and inadequate. He somewhere cites a simile from Ossian, as an example of the superiority of the old poetry to the new, though, even were the historic evidence less convincing, the sentimental melancholy of those poems should be conclusive of their modernness. He had no artistic power such as controls a great work to the serene balance of completeness, but exquisite mechanical skill in the shaping of sentences and paragraphs, or (more rarely) short bits of verse for the expression of a detached thought, sentiment, or image. His works give one the feeling of a sky full of stars,—something impressive and exhilarating certainly, something high overhead and freckled thickly with spots of isolated brightness; but whether these have any mutual relation with each other, or have any concern with our mundane matters, is for the most part matter of conjecture,—astrology as yet, and not astronomy.

It is curious, considering what Thoreau afterwards became, that he was not by nature an observer. He only saw the things he looked for, and was less poet than naturalist. Till he built his Walden shanty, he did not know that the hickory grew in Concord. Till he went to Maine, he had never seen phosphorescent wood, a phenomenon early familiar to most country boys. At forty he speaks of the seeding of the pine as a new discovery, though one should have thought that its gold-dust of blowing pollen might have earlier drawn his eye. Neither his attention nor his genius was of the spontaneous kind. He discovered nothing. He thought everything a discovery of his own, from moonlight to the planting of acorns and nuts by squirrels. This is a defect in his character, but one of his chief charms as a writer. Everything grows fresh under his hand. He delved in his mind and nature; he planted them with all manner of native and foreign seeds, and reaped assiduously. He was not merely solitary, he would be isolated, and succeeded at last in almost persuading himself that he was autochthonous. He valued everything in proportion as he fancied it to be exclusively his own. He complains in "Walden," that there is no one in Concord with whom he could talk of Oriental literature, though the man was living within two miles of his hut who had introduced him to it. This intellectual selfishness becomes sometimes almost painful in reading him. He lacked that generosity of "communication" which Johnson admired in Burke. De Quincey tells us that Wordsworth was impatient when any one else spoke of mountains, as if he had a peculiar property in them. And we can readily understand why it should be so: no one is satisfied with another's appreciation of his mistress. But Thoreau seems to have prized a lofty way of thinking (often we should be inclined to call it a remote one) not so much because it was good in itself as because he wished few to share it with him. It seems now and then as if he did not seek to lure others up "above our lower region of turmoil," but to leave his own name cut on the mountain peak as the first climber. This itch of originality infects his thought and style. To be misty is not to be mystic. He turns commonplaces end for end, and fancies it makes something new of them. As we walk down Park Street, our eye is caught by Dr. Windship's dumb-bells, one of which bears an inscription testifying that it is the heaviest ever put up at arm's length by any athlete; and in reading Mr. Thoreau's books we cannot help feeling as if he sometimes invited our attention to a particular sophism or paradox as the biggest yet maintained by any single writer. He seeks, at all risks, for perversity of thought, and revives the age of *concetti* while he fancies himself going back to a pre-classical nature. "A day," he says, "passed in the society of those Greek sages, such as described in the Banquet of Xenophon, would not be comparable with the dry wit of decayed cranberry-vines and the fresh Attic salt of the moss-beds." It is not so much the True that he loves as the Out-of-the-Way. As the Brazen Age shows itself in other men by exaggeration of phrase, so in him by extravagance of statement. He wishes always to trump your suit and to *ruff* when you least expect it. Do you love Nature because she is beautiful? He will find a better argument in her ugliness. Are you tired of the artificial man? He instantly dresses you up an ideal in a Penobscot Indian, and attributes to this creature of his otherwise-mindedness as peculiarities things that are common to all woodsmen, white or red, and this simply because he has not studied the pale-faced variety.

This notion of an absolute originality, as if one could have a patent-right in it, is an absurdity. A man cannot escape in thought, any more than he can in language, from the past and the present. As no one ever invents a word, and yet language somehow grows by general contribution and necessity, so it is with thought. Mr. Thoreau seems to us to insist in public on going back to flint and steel, when there is a matchbox in his pocket which he knows very well how to use at a pinch. Originality consists in power of digesting and assimilating thought, so that they become part of our life and substance. Montaigne, for example, is one of the most original of authors, though he helped himself to ideas in every direction. But they turn to blood and coloring in his style, and give a freshness of complexion that is forever charming. In Thoreau much seems yet to be foreign and unassimilated, showing itself in symptoms of indigestion. A preacher up of Nature, we now and then detect under the surly and stoic garb something of the sophist and the sentimentalizer. We are far from implying that this was conscious on his part. But it is much easier for a man to impose on himself when he measures only with himself. A greater familiarity with ordinary men would have done Thoreau good, by showing him how many fine qualities are common to the race. The radical vice of his theory of life was, that he confounded physical with spiritual remoteness from men. One is far enough withdrawn from his fellows if he keep himself clear of their weaknesses. He is not so truly withdrawn as exiled, if he refuse to share in their strength. It is a morbid self-consciousness that pronounces the world of men empty and worthless before trying it, the instinctive evasion of one who is sensible of some innate weakness, and retorts the accusation of it before any has made it but himself. To a healthy mind, the world is a constant challenge of opportunity. Mr. Thoreau had not a healthy mind, or he would not have been so fond of prescribing. His whole life was a search for the doctor. The old mystics had a wiser sense of what the world was worth. They ordained a severe apprenticeship to law and even ceremonial, in order to the gaining of freedom and mastery over these. Seven years of service for Rachel were to be rewarded at last with Leah. Seven other years of faithfulness with her were to win them at last the true bride of their souls. Active Life was with them the only path to the Contemplative.

Thoreau had no humor, and this implies that he was a sorry logician. Himself an artist in rhetoric, he confounds thought with style when he undertakes to speak of the latter. He was forever talking of getting away from the world, but he must be always

near enough to it, nay, to the Concord corner of it, to feel the
impression he makes there. He verifies the shrewd remark of Sainte-
Beuve, "On touche encore à son temps et très-fort, même quand
on le repousee." This egotism of his is a Stylites pillar after all,
a seclusion which keeps him in the public eye. The dignity of man
is an excellent thing, but therefore to hold one's self too sacred
and precious is the reverse of excellent. There is something de-
lightfully absurd in six volumes addressed to a world of such
"vulgar fellows" as Thoreau affirmed his fellow-men to be. We once
had a glimpse of a genuine solitary who spent his winters one
hundred and fifty miles beyond all human communication, and
there dwelt with his rifle as his only confidant. Compared with this,
the shanty on Walden Pond has something the air, it must be confessed, of the Hermitage of La Chevrette. We do not believe that
the way to a true cosmopolitanism carries one into the woods or the
society of musquashes. Perhaps the narrowest provincialism is that
of Self; that of Kleinwinkel is nothing to it. The natural man, like
the singing birds, comes out of the forest as inevitably as the
natural bear and the wildcat stick there. To seek to be natural
implies a consciousness that forbids all naturalness forever. It is
as easy—and no easier—to be natural in a *salon* as in a swamp,
if one do not aim at it, for what we call unnaturalness always has
its spring in a man's thinking too much about himself. "It is impossible," said Turgot, "for a vulgar man to be simple."

We look upon a great deal of the modern sentimentalism about
Nature as a mark of disease. It is one more symptom of the general
liver-complaint. In a man of wholesome constitution the wilderness
is well enough for a mood or a vacation, but not for a habit of life.
Those who have most loudly advertised their passion for seclusion
and their intimacy with nature, from Petrarch down, have been
mostly sentimentalists, unreal men, misanthropes on the spindle side,
solacing an uneasy suspicion of themselves by professing contempt
for their kind. They make demands on the world in advance pro-
portioned to their inward measure of their own merit, and are
angry that the world pays only by the visible measure of perform-
ance. It is true of Rousseau, the modern founder of the sect, true
of St. Pierre, his intellectual child, and of Chateaubriand, his
grandchild, the inventor of what we may call the primitive forest
cure, and who first was touched by the solemn falling of a tree
from natural decay in the windless silence of the woods. It is a
very shallow view that affirms trees and rocks to be healthy, and
cannot see that men in communities are just as true to the laws of

their organization and destiny; that can tolerate the puffin and the
fox, but not the fool and the knave; that would shun politics because of its demagogues, and snuff up the stench of the obscene
fungus. The divine life of Nature is more wonderful, more various,
more sublime in man than in any other of her works, and the
wisdom that is gained by commerce with men, as Montaigne and
Shakespeare gained it, or with one's own soul among men, as
Dante, is the most delightful, as it is the most precious, of all. In
outward nature it is still man that interests us, and we care far
less for the things seen than the way in which poetic eyes like
Wordsworth's or Thoreau's see them, and the reflections they cast
there. To hear the to-do that is often made over the simple fact
that a man sees the image of himself in the outward world, one is reminded of a savage when he for the first time catches a glimpse
of himself in a looking-glass. "Venerable child of Nature," we are
tempted to say, "to whose science in the invention of the tobacco-
pipe, to whose art in the tattooing of thine undegenerate hide not
yet enslaved by tailors, we are slowly striving to climb back, the
miracle thou beholdest is sold in my unhappy country for a
shilling!" If matters go on as they have done, and everybody must
needs blab of all the favors that have been done him by roadside
and river-brink and woodland walk, as if to kiss and tell were no
longer treachery, it will be a positive refreshment to meet a man
who is as superbly indifferent to Nature as she is to him. By and
by we shall have John Smith, of No. –12, –12th Street, advertising
that he is not the J. S. who saw a cow-lily on Thursday last, as
he never saw one in his life; would not see one if he could, and is
prepared to prove an alibi on the day in question.

Solitary communion with Nature does not seem to have been
sanitary or sweetening in its influence on Thoreau's character. On
the contrary, his letters show him more cynical as he grew older.
While he studied with respectful attention the minks and wood-
chucks, his neighbors, he looked with utter contempt on the august
drama of destiny of which his country was the scene, and on which
the curtain had already risen. He was converting us back to a
state of nature "so eloquently," as Voltaire said of Rousseau, "that
he almost persuaded us to go on all fours," while the wiser fates
were making it possible for us to walk erect for the first time. Had
he conversed more with his fellows, his sympathies would have
widened with the assurance that his peculiar genius had more
appreciation, and his writings a larger circle of readers, or at least
a warmer one, than he dreamed of. We have the highest tes-

timony * to the natural sweetness, sincerity, and nobleness of his temper, and in his books an equally irrefragable one to the rare quality of his mind. He was not a strong thinker, but a sensitive feeler. Yet his mind strikes us as cold and wintry in its purity. A light snow has fallen everywhere where he seems to come on the track of the shier sensations that would elsewhere leave no trace. We think greater compression would have done more for his fame. A feeling of sameness comes over us as we read so much. Trifles are recorded with an over-minute punctuality and conscientiousness of detail. We cannot help thinking sometimes of the man who

> "watches, starves, freezes, and sweats
> To learn but catechisms and alphabets
> Of unconcerning things, matters of fact,"

and sometimes of the saying of the Persian poet, that "when the owl would boast, he boasts of catching mice at the edge of a hole." We could readily part with some of his affectations. It was well enough for Pythagoras to say, once for all, "When I was Euphorbus at the siege of Troy"; not so well for Thoreau to travesty it into "When I was a shepherd on the plains of Assyria." A naive thing said over again is anything but naive. But with every exception, there is no writing comparable with Thoreau's in kind, that is comparable with it in degree where it is best; where it disengages itself, that is, from the tangled roots and dead leaves of a second-hand Orientalism, and runs limpid and smooth and broadening as it runs, a mirror for whatever is grand and lovely in both worlds.

George Sand says neatly, that "Art is not a study of positive reality," (*actuality* were the fitter word,) "but a seeking after ideal truth." It would be doing very inadequate justice to Thoreau if we left it to be inferred that this ideal element did not exist in him, and that too in larger proportion, if less obtrusive, than his nature-worship. He took nature as the mountain-path to an ideal world. If the path wind a good deal, if he record too faithfully every trip over a root, if he botanize somewhat wearisomely, he gives us now and then superb outlooks from some jutting crag, and brings us out at last into an illimitable ether, where the breathing is not difficult for those who have any true touch of the climbing spirit. His shanty-life was a mere impossibility, so far as his own conception of it goes, as an entire independency of mankind. The tub

---

* Mr. Emerson, in the Biographical Sketch prefixed to the "Excursions."

of Diogenes had a sounder bottom. Thoreau's experiment actually
presupposed all that complicated civilization which it theoretically
abjured. He squatted on another man's land; he borrows an axe;
his boards, his nails, his bricks, his mortar, his books, his lamp, his
fish-hooks, his plough, his hoe, all turn state's evidence against him
as an accomplice in the sin of that artificial civilization which
rendered it possible that such a person as Henry D. Thoreau
should exist at all. *Magnis tamen excidit ausis.* His aim was a
noble and a useful one, in the direction of "plain living and high
thinking." It was a practical sermon on Emerson's text that "things
are in the saddle and ride mankind," an attempt to solve Carlyle's
problem of "lessening your denominator." His whole life was a
rebuke of the waste and aimlessness of our American luxury, which
is an abject enslavement to tawdry upholstery. He had "fine
translunary things" in him. His better style as a writer is in keeping with the simplicity and purity of his life. We have said that
his range was narrow, but to be a master is to be a master. He had
caught his English at its living source, among the poets and prose-
writers of its best days; his literature was extensive and recondite;
his quotations are always nuggets of the purest ore; there are
sentences of his as perfect as anything in the language, and
thoughts as clearly crystallized; his metaphors and images are always fresh from the soil; he had watched Nature like a detective
who is to go upon the stand; as we read him, it seems as if all-out-
of-doors had kept a diary and become its own Montaigne; we look
at the landscape as in a Claude Lorraine glass; compared with his,
all other books of similar aim, even White's Selborne, seem dry
as a country clergyman's meteorological journal in an old almanac.
He belongs with Donne and Browne and Novalis; if not with the
originally creative men, with the scarcely smaller class who are
peculiar, and whose leaves shed their invisible thought-seed like
ferns.

H. A. Page [Alexander H. Japp]

[The Walden Motive]

The retreat to Walden has led to much misunderstanding,—to the charge that Thoreau was a morbid egotist, a sentimentalist, a solitary; a charge which has been boldly repeated, recently, by high authorities, who should have known better. Nothing could well be further from the truth. He was not always logically consistent in his utterances, and, indeed, did not aim at being so; but, amid all his *brusquerie*, we detect the note of real interest in humanity and in human affairs. Only, you must not bore him with minor details of tap-room gossip, or with the news of the cliques. It was, indeed, against *cliquerie* and all forms of false and half-hearted association that he had taken up his parable; and when he retired to Walden he almost tells in his own words that he unconsciously acted on the axiom of Goethe, "When I need to recruit my strength I must retire into solitude." But neither with Thoreau nor with Goethe could that solitude be a period of inertia, of weak self-pity, or of brooding discontent; it must have its own activities, its own interests with a genuine restoring charm caught from Nature. Were this missed, all was missed. The Walden episode is not seen truly until it is viewed in relation to the whole scope and purpose of Thoreau's life. What led him to Walden determined his attitude to human institutions; and the same experiment, in a less striking form, was carried on to the end. Thoreau went to Walden not to escape men, but to prepare himself for them, and, as far as he could, for the artificial conventions on which society necessarily rests; not to brood, but to act—only to act in lines that would enable him to stand for ever after—free, vigorous, independent. There is a strange, close-packed realism in his writing, in large measure derived from this, a realism thoroughly symptomatic of the man and his character, as though he specially followed Nature in her economy of seed-packing; and it should be observed that you never get a hint of the recluse, who speedily falls to dreaming and vain pitying of himself. There is no self-pity in Thoreau, rather a robust self-sufficiency that could claim the privilege of rendering manly help, though never seeking

Reprinted from *Thoreau: His Life and Aims* (Boston: James R. Osgood & Company, 1877), pp. 108–12.

29

or accepting any, and that loves to administer readily what Emerson calls 'shocks of effort.' But there was in him nothing of the rebel proper; he delighted above all things to be at home, and to reverence, only you must allow him something of his own way. When he refused to pay taxes after Government followed him to the forest, it was out of no abstract opposition or dislike to society, —he was the last man to act from sentiment; he asserted that there was still a sphere where Government had no right to follow if a man could only find and fix it, and where it did despite to itself by the assertion of its power.

Something is also to be said for the circumstances amid which he was cast. Instead of being a solitary, he was more than usually sensitive to influences operating around him. Indeed, it is the consciousness of a necessity to resist that imparts the tone which has been mistaken for morbid. When the wave of transcendentalism met that of ultra-practicalism,—intensified by the expansion of territory which presented a wider sphere for it to act in,—and threatened to be swallowed up by it, what was left for a faithful disciple but to bear his witness for the individuality which he had learned to value through transcendentalism, but which was now well nigh threatened with extinction? Thoreau's retreat to Walden may have a meaning in this light also. Witnesses, many and powerful, transcendentalism has had; Thoreau is its hermit, if you will, but a hermit who consciously carries society in all its higher interests with him. While his own countrymen with fatal inconsistency have too largely regarded him as a morbid solitary, we in England, if we had not followed them, have erred by conceiving of him as a kind of semi-wild man of the woods, with no reason or order in his procedure, though now and then throwing out fine thoughts, and saved from being a wild man altogether only by a dash of rarer instinct, which made him influential with the lower creatures, but divorced him from human society, if it did not even make him its enemy. Thoreau, instead of being divorced from the spirit of his day, in a special way interpreted it. He would not spend time in trying or experimenting with conventions, which he held had been already sufficiently tested; he would go to the heart of Nature and try to learn for himself some new law there, or at least to see the old laws in direct and clear relation to his own spirit. As others tried it in various forms of association, so he in his convention with Nature, the one experiment, as he held it, being just as valuable as the other. Democracy in a new country must ever be as hard on individuality as aristocracy in an old one:

the problem is to maintain that intact, and do no despite to others in the process. The very presence of society limits your freedom of action; it may be well to learn freedom apart, that even the self-control due to society may have real value in it, and not be automatic merely. Mechanical arrangements are the death of all true society: let us learn to dispense with them, or to consider them at least non-essential.

There is a social and moral regeneration, for the want of which it may be said that, at certain crises, the world becomes inert and sick. For this disease there may be many medicines: socialism may contribute its quota of relief; and practical political reforms rightly directed may do a little. Let us one and all be true to ourselves first, said Thoreau, and cherish whatever instincts and impulses are sent to us direct from Nature. Then we may return to practical and social life, pure if not strong, with a capacity as of genius, to relieve ourselves from the tyranny of social pre-occupations and self-occupying thoughts, of which thousands daily die, or doom themselves to a living death, strangled as if by Lilliputian cords. He believed with his whole soul, like Wordsworth, in the fountains that are within. Returning thus to the demands of busy life, he held that we should have capacities of enjoyment and service more than doubled,—fitted to be at once true citizens, true to ourselves, faithful reformers, very jealous of what is accepted merely by authority or for its newness; ready to return on the simplest principles of right and to defend them.

Robert Louis Stevenson

Henry David Thoreau:
His Character and Opinions

I

Thoreau's thin, penetrating, big-nosed face, even in a bad woodcut, conveys some hint of the limitations of his mind and character.

Reprinted from *Cornhill Magazine,* XLI (June 1880), 665–82.

With his almost acid sharpness of insight, with his almost animal dexterity in act, there went none of that large, unconscious geniality of the world's heroes. He was not easy, not ample, not urbane, not even kind; his enjoyment was hardly smiling, or the smile was not broad enough to be convincing; he had no waste lands nor kitchen-midden in his nature, but was all improved and sharpened to a point. "He was bred to no profession," says Emerson; "he never married, he lived alone; he never went to church; he never voted; he refused to pay a tax to the state; he ate no flesh, he drank no wine, he never knew the use of tobacco; and, though a naturalist, he used neither trap nor gun. When asked at dinner what dish he preferred, he answered, 'The nearest.' " So many negative superiorities begin to smack a little of the prig. From his later works he was in the habit of cutting out humorous passages, under the impression that they were beneath the dignity of his moral muse; and there we see the prig stand public and confessed. It was "much easier," says Emerson, acutely, much easier for Thoreau to say *no* than *yes;* and that is a characteristic which depicts the man. It is a useful accompaniment to be able to say *no*, but surely it is the essence of amiability to prefer to say *yes* where it is possible. There is something wanting in the man who does not hate himself whenever he is constrained to say no. And there was a great deal wanting in this born dissenter. He was almost shockingly devoid of weaknesses; he had not enough of them to be truly polar with humanity; whether you call him demi-god or demi-man, he was at least not altogether one of us, for he was not touched with a feeling of our infirmities. The world's heroes have room for all positive qualities, even those which are disreputable, in the capacious theatre of their dispositions. Such can live many lives; while a Thoreau can live but one, and that only with perpetual foresight.

He was no ascetic, rather an Epicurean of the nobler sort; and he had this one great merit, that he succeeded so far as to be happy. "I love my fate to the core and rind," he wrote once; and even while he lay dying, here is what he dictated (for it seems he was already too feeble to control the pen): "You ask particularly after my health. I *suppose* that I have not many months to live, but of course know nothing about it. I may say that I am enjoying existence as much as ever, and regret nothing." It is not given to all to bear so clear a testimony to the sweetness of their fate, nor to any without courage and wisdom; for this world in itself is but a painful and uneasy place of residence, and lasting happiness, at least to the self-conscious, comes only from within. Now, Thoreau's content and ectasy in living was, we may say, like a plant that he had watered and tended with womanish solicitude; for there is apt to be something unmanly, something almost dastardly, in a life that does not move with dash and freedom, and that fears the bracing contact of the world. In one word, Thoreau was a skulker. He did not wish virtue to go out of him among his fellow-men, but slunk into a corner to hoard it for himself. He left all for the sake of certain virtuous self-indulgences. It is true that his tastes were noble; that his ruling passion was to keep himself unspotted from the world; and that his luxuries were all of the same healthy order as cold tubs and early rising. But a man may be both coldly cruel in the pursuit of goodness, and morbid even in the pursuit of health. I cannot lay my hands on the passage in which he explains his abstinence from tea and coffee, but I am sure I have the meaning correctly. It is this: He thought it bad economy and worthy of no true virtuoso to spoil the natural rapture of the morning with such muddy stimulants; let him but see the sun rise, and he was already sufficiently inspirited for the labors of the day. That may be reason good enough to abstain from tea; but when we go on to find the same man, on the same or similar grounds, abstain from nearly everything that his neighbors innocently and pleasurably use, and from the rubs and trials of human society itself into the bargain, we recognize that valetudinarian healthfulness which is more delicate than sickness itself. We need have no respect for a state of artificial training. True health is to be able to do without it. Shakespeare, we can imagine, might begin the day upon a quart of ale, and yet enjoy the sunrise to the full as much as Thoreau, and commemorate his enjoyment in vastly better verses. A man *compare* who must separate himself from his neighbors' habits in order to *with* be happy, is in much the same case with one who requires to take *today* opium for the same purpose. What we want to see is one who can breast into the world, do a man's work, and still preserve his first and pure enjoyment of existence.

Thoreau's faculties were of a piece with his moral shyness; for they were all delicacies. He could guide himself about the woods on the darkest night by the touch of his feet. He could pick up an exact dozen of pencils by the feeling, pace distances with accuracy, and gauge cubic contents by the eye. His smell was so dainty that he could perceive the fetor of dwelling-houses as he passed them by at night; his palate so unsophisticated that, like a child, he disliked the taste of wine—or perhaps, living in America, had never tasted any that was good; and his knowledge of nature was so complete and curious that he could have told the time of year, within a day or so, by the aspect of the plants. In his dealings with animals, he was the original of Hawthorne's Donatello. He pulled the woodchuck out of its hole by the tail; the hunted fox came to him for protection; wild squirrels have been seen to nestle in his waistcoat; he would thrust his arm into a pool and bring forth a bright, panting fish, lying undismayed in the palm of his hand. There were few things that he could not do. He could make a house, a boat, a pencil, or a book. He was a surveyor, a scholar, a natural historian. He could run, walk, climb, skate, swim and manage a boat. The smallest occasion served to display his physical accomplishment; and a manufacturer from merely observing his dexterity with the window of a railway carriage, offered him a situation on the spot. "The only fruit of much living," he observes, "is the ability to do some slight thing better." But such was the exactitude of his senses, so alive was he in every fibre, that it seems as if the maxim should be changed in his case, for he could do most things with unusual perfection. And perhaps he had an approving eye to himself when he wrote: "Though the youth at last grows indifferent, the laws of the universe are not indifferent, *but are forever on the side of the most sensitive.*"

II

Thoreau had decided, it would seem, from the very first to lead a life of self-improvement: the needle did not tremble as with richer natures, but pointed steadily north; and as he saw duty and inclination in one, he turned all his strength in that direction. He was met upon the threshold by a common difficulty. In this world, in spite of its many agreeable features, even the most sensitive must undergo some drudgery to live. It is not possible to devote your time to study and meditation without what are quaintly but happily denominated private means; these absent, a man must contrive to earn his bread by some service to the public such as the public cares to pay him for; or, as Thoreau loved to put it, Apollo must serve Admetus. This was to Thoreau even a sourer necessity than it is to most; there was a love of freedom, a strain of the wild man, in his nature, that rebelled with violence against the yoke of custom; and he was so eager to cultivate himself and to be happy in his own society, that he could consent with difficulty even to the interruptions of friendship. "*Such are my engagements to my-*

self that I dare not promise," he once wrote in answer to an invitation; and the italics are his own. Marcus Aurelius found time to study virtue, and between whiles to conduct the imperial affairs of Rome; but Thoreau is so busy improving himself, that he must think twice about a morning call. And now imagine him condemned for eight hours a day to some uncongenial and unmeaning business! He shrank from the very look of the mechanical in life; all should if possible, be sweetly spontaneous and swimmingly progressive. Thus he learned to make lead-pencils, and, when he had gained the best certificate and his friends began to congratulate him on his establishment in life, calmly announced that he should never make another. "Why should I?" he said; "I would not do again what I have done once." For when a thing has once been done as well as it wants to be, it is of no further interest to the self-improver. Yet in after years, and when it became needful to support his family, he returned patiently to this mechanical art—a step more than worthy of himself.

The pencils seem to have been Apollo's first experiment in the service of Admetus; but others followed. "I have thoroughly tried school-keeping," he writes, "and found that my expenses were in proportion, or rather out of proportion, to my income; for I was obliged to dress and train, not to say think and believe, accordingly, and I lost my time into the bargain. As I did not teach for the benefit of my fellow-men, but simply for a livelihood, this was a failure. I have tried trade; but I found that it would take ten years to get under way in that, and that then I should probably be on my way to the devil." Nothing, indeed, can surpass his scorn for all so-called business. Upon that subject, gall squirts from him at a touch. "The whole enterprise of this nation is not illustrated by a thought," he writes; "it is not warmed by a sentiment; there is nothing in it for which a man should lay down his life, nor even his gloves." And again: "If our merchants did not most of them fail, and the banks too, my faith in the old laws of this world would be staggered. The statement that ninety-six in a hundred doing such business surely break down is perhaps the sweetest fact that statistics have revealed." The wish was probably father to the figures; but there is something enlivening in a hatred of so genuine a brand, hot as Corsican revenge and sneering like Voltaire.

Pencils, school-keeping, and trade being thus discarded one after another, Thoreau, with a stroke of strategy, turned the position. He saw his way to get his board and lodging for practically nothing; and Admetus never got less work out of any servant since

the world began. It was his ambition to be an Oriental philosopher;
but he was always a very Yankee sort of Oriental. Even in the
peculiar attitude in which he stood to money, his system of personal economics, as we may call it, he displayed a vast amount of
truly down-east calculation, and he adopted poverty like a piece
of business. Yet his system is based on one or two ideas which,
I believe, come naturally to all thoughtful youths, and are only
pounded out of them by city uncles. Indeed, something essentially
youthful distinguishes all Thoreau's knock-down blows at current
opinion. Like the posers of a child, they leave the orthodox in a
kind of speechless agony. These know the thing is nonsense. They
are sure there must be an answer, yet somehow cannot find it. So
it is with his system of economy. He cuts through the subject on
so new a plane that the accepted arguments apply no longer; he
attacks it in a new dialect where there are no catchwords ready
made for the defender; after you have been boxing for years on a
polite, gladiatorial convention, here is an assailant who does not
scruple to hit below the belt.

"The cost of a thing," says he, "is *the amount of what I will
call life* which is required to be exchanged for it, immediately or
in the long run." I have been accustomed to put it to myself, perhaps more clearly, that the price we have to pay for money is paid
in liberty. Between these two ways of it, at least, the reader will
probably not fail to find a third definition of his own; and it follows, on one or other, that a man may pay too dearly for his livelihood, by giving, in Thoreau's terms, his whole life for it, or, in
mine, bartering for it the whole of his available liberty, and becoming a slave till death. There are two questions to be considered—
the quality of what we buy, and the price we have to pay for it.
Do you want a thousand a year, a two thousand a year, or a ten
thousand a year livelihood? and can you afford the one you want?
It is a matter of taste; it is not in the least degree a question of
duty, though commonly supposed so. But there is no authority
for that view anywhere. It is nowhere in the Bible. It is true that
we might do a vast amount of good if we were wealthy, but it is
also highly improbable; not many do; and the art of growing rich
is not only quite distinct from that of doing good, but the practice of the one does not at all train a man for practising the other.
"Money might be of great service to me," writes Thoreau; "but
the difficulty now is that I do not improve my opportunities, and
therefore I am not prepared to have my opportunities increased."
It is a mere illusion that, above a certain income, the personal

desires will be satisfied and leave a wider margin for the generous impulse. It is as difficult to be generous, or anything else, except perhaps a member of Parliament, on thirty thousand as on two hundred a year.

Now Thoreau's tastes were well defined. He loved to be free, to be master of his time and seasons, to indulge the mind rather than the body; he preferred long rambles to rich dinners, his own reflections to the consideration of society, and an easy, calm, unfettered, active life among green trees to dull toiling at the counter of a bank. And such being his inclination he determined to gratify it. A poor man must save off something; he determined to save off his livelihood. "When a man has attained those things which are necessary to life," he writes, "there is another alternative than to obtain the superfluities; *he may adventure on life now,* his vacation from humbler toil having commenced." Thoreau would get shelter, some kind of covering for his body, and necessary daily bread; even these he should get as cheaply as possible; and then, his vacation from humbler toil having commenced, devote himself to Oriental philosophers, the study of nature, and the work of self-improvement.

Prudence, which bids us all go to the ant for wisdom and hoard against the day of sickness, was not a favorite with Thoreau. He preferred that other, whose name is so much misappropriated, Faith. When he had secured the necessaries of the moment, he would not reckon up possible accidents or torment himself with trouble for the future. He had no toleration for the man "who ventures to live only by the aid of the mutual insurance company, which has promised to bury him decently." He would trust himself a little to the world. "We may safely trust a good deal more than we do," says he. "How much is not done by us! or what if we had been taken sick?" And then, with a stab of satire, he describes contemporary mankind in a phrase: "All the day long on the alert, at night we unwillingly say our prayers and commit ourselves to uncertainties." It is not likely that the public will be much affected by Thoreau, when they blink the direct injunctions of the religion they profess; and yet, whether we will or no, we make the same hazardous ventures; we back our own health and the honesty of our neighbors for all that we are worth; and it is chilling to think how many must lose their wager.

In 1845, twenty-eight years old, an age by which the liveliest have usually declined into some conformity with the world, Thoreau, with a capital of something less than five pounds and a borrowed axe, walked forth into the woods by Walden Pond, and began his new experiment in life. He built himself a dwelling, and returned the axe, he says with characteristic and workmanlike pride, sharper than when he borrowed it; he reclaimed a patch, where he cultivated beans, peas, potatoes, and sweet corn; he had his bread to bake, his farm to dig, and for the matter of six weeks in the summer he worked at surveying, carpentry, or some other of his numerous dexterities, for hire. For more than five years, this was all that he required for his support, and he had the winter and most of the summer at his entire disposal. For six weeks of occupation, a little cooking and a little hygienic gardening, the man, you may say, had as good as stolen his livelihood. Or we must rather allow that he had done far better; for the thief himself is continually and busily occupied; and even one born to inherit a million will have more calls upon his time than Thoreau. Well might he say, "What old people tell you you cannot do, you try and find you can." And how surprising is his conclusion: "I am convinced that *to maintain one's self on this earth is not a hardship, but a pastime*, if we will live simply and wisely; *as the pursuits of simpler nations are still the sports of the more artificial*."

When he had enough of that kind of life, he showed the same simplicity in giving it up as in beginning it. There are some who could have done the one, but, vanity forbidding, not the other; and that is perhaps the story of the hermits; but Thoreau made no fetich of his own example, and did what he wanted squarely. And five years is long enough for an experiment and to prove the success of transcendental Yankeeism. It is not his frugality which is worthy of note; for, to begin with, that was inborn, and therefore inimitable by others who are differently constituted; and again, it was no new thing, but has often been equalled by poor Scotch students at the universities. The point is the sanity of his view of life, and the insight with which he recognized the position of money, and thought out for himself the problem of riches and a livelihood. Apart from his eccentricities, he had perceived, and was acting on, a truth of universal application. For money enters in two different characters into the scheme of life. A certain amount, varying with the number and empire of our desires, is a true necessary to each one of us in the present order of society; but beyond that amount, money is a commodity to be bought or not to be bought, a luxury in which we may either indulge or stint ourselves, like any other. And there are many luxuries that we may legitimately prefer to it, such as a grateful conscience, a country life, or the woman of our inclination. Trite, flat, and obvious as this conclusion may appear, we have only to look round us in society to see how scantily it has been recognized; and perhaps even ourselves, after a little reflection, may decide to spend a trifle less for money, and indulge ourselves a trifle more in the article of freedom. . . .

Thoreau's true subject was the pursuit of self-improvement combined with an unfriendly criticism of life as it goes on in our societies; it is there that he best displays the freshness and surprising trenchancy of his intellect; it is there that his style becomes plain and vigorous, and therefore, according to his own formula, ornamental. Yet he did not care to follow this vein singly, but must drop into it by the way in books of a different purport. *Walden, or Life in the Woods, A Week on the Concord and Merrimack Rivers, The Maine Woods*, such are the titles he affects. He was probably reminded by his delicate critical perception that the true business of literature is with narrative; in reasoned narrative, and there alone, that art enjoys all its advantages, and suffers least from its defects. Dry precept and disembodied disquisition, as they can only be read with an effort of abstraction, can never convey a complete or perfectly natural impression. Truth, even in literature, must be clothed with flesh and blood, or it cannot tell its whole story to the reader. Hence the effect of anecdote on simple minds; and hence good biographies and works of high, imaginative art are not only far more entertaining, but far more edifying, than books of theory or precept. Now, Thoreau could not clothe his opinions in the garment of art, for that was not his talent; but he sought to gain the same elbow-room for himself, and to afford a similar relief to his readers, by mingling his thoughts with a record of experience. . . .

3. Twentieth-Century Readings

Norman Foerster

The Humanism of Thoreau

... Thus, as Thoreau roamed over his Concord countryside, he was, as he knew at bottom, becoming acquainted with himself, with the spiritual universe latent in him as in every man, and not simply with outward nature. This spiritual universe he looked upon as static, fixed for all time, as in Plato, so that his task was to come to know it, rather than, as in the contemporary German philosophy, to create it for himself. He could write, in the German way, "This world is but a canvas to our imaginations"; yet his was no world-positing ego—instinctively, if he had understood Fichte and his followers, he would have shunned that invitation to excess, to infinite longing, to indulgence in the nauseating delights of the lower ranges of human emotion. The idea of correspondence, indeed, meant in his case a veritable discipline. Nature will not reveal man to himself unless he fits himself to perceive the correspondence. He is to rely, not on the outer world of nature, but on his own inner nature—"the pond will not seem like a mountain tarn, but a low pool, a silent muddy water, a place for fishermen." He knew that he could not get the better of nature, drive a shrewd Yankee bargain with such as she: here, as in political economy, he says, supply answers to demand. "Nature does not cast pearls before swine. There is just as much beauty visible to us in the landscape as we are prepared to appreciate—not a grain more." He proceeds to explain this by reminding us of the familiar truth that different persons see different objects in nature, that you see mainly what you are looking for, that when you have once become familiar with the idea, or image, of a plant, for example, you can hardly see anything else. Nature's supply depends on your demand, your fitness to receive. This view accounts, in part, for the discipline of the will and mind to which Thoreau made himself submit.

Depreciating the actual, he asserts roundly that "our thoughts are the epochs in our lives: all else is but as a journal of the winds that blew while we were here." The truly rich man, he says, is he who finds delight in his own thoughts. Such were the Hindus, with

Reprinted from *The Nation*, CV (July 5, 1917), 9–12, by permission of the author.

their perpetual contemplation. Such was he himself, when the gods were kind. "If I am visited by a thought, I chew that cud each successive morning, as long as there is any flavor in it. Until my keepers shake down some fresh fodder." His life at Walden offered a perfect opportunity for reflection, and well did he use it. Some of his pleasantest hours there, he tells us, were during the interminable rain-storms of spring and autumn, when, confined to his hut, he enjoyed a long evening memorable in its soothing roar of the elements and its sense of solitude, "in which many thoughts had time to take root and unfold themselves." No doubt his thinking assumed various forms: more often syllogistic than Emerson's, it was also more fanciful, and, if not so elevated, was perhaps more flexible. Not often was it idle, inchoate dreaming. There was a backbone in his mind, so to speak, that would bend but not yield completely. Though clothed in images, his thoughts were not the disordered dream of the nerveless sentimentalist, but shone before him bright as the world of the Greek. His mind had clarity, delicacy, grasp, penetration, masculine energy, as his books show. The man who wrote "Walden" was not given to empty revery, but to genuine reflection and contemplation.

Wittingly beset by the tyranny of observation, Thoreau welcomed occasions that encouraged thinking. Walking by night had at least this advantage, he found, that moonlight is more favorable to reflection than sunlight. "The intense light of the sun unfits me for meditation, makes me wander in my thought; my life is too diffuse and dissipated." Again, he liked certain unseasonable days in midsummer, when "the coolness concentrated your thought." Solitude, again, invited fruitful brooding, as society did not, and he was therefore glad to spend most of his days apart from men. Observation and reflection together succeeded in worsting the hobgoblin of solitude—a miserable loneliness; for only once in the Walden solitude did Thoreau experience an unpleasant sense of being alone, and then but "for an hour." The solitude of winter he rejoiced in, the "dear privacy and retirement and solitude which winter makes possible"! That was his favorite season, if he had one, and first of all it stood for the inward life, as his italics suggest: "Winter, with its *inwardness*, is upon us. A man is constrained to sit down, and to think." Far from needing a rich, glowing landscape, he was deeply satisfied with the cold and barren splendors of winter and of autumn—for "November Eat-heart" was also very dear to him. He relished a November day such "as will almost oblige a man to eat his own heart.... Ah, but is not this a glorious time for your deep inward fires?" He liked to assert that his inward wealth was in steadfast proportion to the outward poverty and dreariness, and doubtless we may believe him. But, after all, there is an occasion for reflection superior to any of those already mentioned. Thinking he viewed sometimes as the clearing-house for impressions, or "influences," more or less unconsciously gathered in his converse with the outer world; and he was wise enough to recognize that the best place for this clarification was within doors. "Out of doors," he confesses, "my thought is commonly drowned, as it were, and shrunken, pressed down by stupendous piles of light ethereal influences, for the pressure of the atmosphere is still fifteen pounds to a square inch. I can do little more than preserve my equilibrium and resist the pressure of the atmosphere. I can only nod like the rye-heads in the breeze. I expand more surely in my chamber, as far as expression goes, as if that pressure were taken off; but here outdoors is the place to store influences." His expression expands, he means, of course, because his mind contracts, concentrates. If expansive, partly obedient to the currents of nature, when out of doors, he concentrated within doors, allying himself with that greater stream of the eternities—"The stream I love unbounded flows," to use the phrase of his friend Emerson. In the presence of nature, he prized sounds; in his chamber, silence, "the communing of a conscious soul with itself." Sound, he remarks, is when we hear outwardly, silence when we hear inwardly. Silence, like nearly everything that he rated highly, is thus of man, not of nature: "It takes a man to make a room silent," or, he might have added, to make nature silent.

Despite all his observation, despite the acuteness of his perceptive faculties, he was an ardent votary of what he termed "a kind of Brahminical, Artesian, Inner Temple life." It pleased him to contrast his own piety with the brazen triviality of his fellow-men, who toiled and chattered and bargained and cheated and wallowed in the actual, while he found joy, peace, and certainty in the unchanging real. While they sent forth their "confused *tintin-nabulum*," he hearkened to the still voices of Silence and Solitude, and came to his bearings. He was a *Doppelgänger* with a difference, for the part of him that, as he says, was spectator to the rest, ironically forming its own opinions and uttering them, was the universal spirit, "no more I than it is you." Instead of being "wholly involved in Nature," he was subservient to the spirit within. This, and not nature, was the inspirer that he referred to when he suggested that, if he did not keep pace with his companions, it was because he heard a different drummer.

His was no gospel of loafing and inviting the soul. Instead of merely inviting the soul, he would go to bring her, and instead of loafing, he would work unceasingly. *This* was his gospel, rather: "Many of our days should be spent, not in vague expectations and lying on our oars, but in carrying out deliberately and faithfully the hundred little purposes which every man's genius must have suggested to him." There was a grim deliberation and an inflexible faithfulness about everything that Thoreau did; he did not lie on his oars and drift with the current, but sat stiffly at the helm, directing his course with, if anything, an excess of concentration. He knew, if no one else did, where he was going, and in his mastery had a lively contempt for the sentimental mode of life, which, as he puts it, does not set a goal before itself and "cannot build a causeway to its objects," but idly "sits on a bank looking over a bog, singing its desires." The tormenting desires of European romanticism—the sighs, the aching void, the meltings, the sweet abandon, the infinite weariness—were more remote from him than was the common-sense of the eighteenth century. Whatever romantic traits he had were held in check by an intellectual attitude that reminds one of the deists, and an emotional attitude that reminds one of the Puritans.

"All wisdom is the reward of a discipline, conscious or unconscious"; "That aim in life is highest which requires the highest and finest discipline"—in such remarks do we come very close to the essential Thoreau. The straight and narrow way of right living is indicated by one's "genius," or inner light. Obey your genius—obey it fully—and you have submitted to the sternest of taskmasters. Thoreau, at least, did not ask, "What do I desire?" but "What *ought* I to desire—what does that heart of flame within me, unconcerned, disinterested as a judge, demand of me?" So soon as he saw his goal, he proceeded thitherward without rest or deviation.

The goal, of course, was always an inward one. While the sentimentalist tried to escape from his self—losing his sense of separateness by immersion in outward nature, or in the life of a past time, or in the rapt harmony of music, Thoreau unflinchingly stared his self in the face, and studied it. "The art of life! . . . By what disciplines to secure the most life, with what care to watch our thoughts. To observe what transpires, not in the street, but in the mind and heart of me!" Never, in one sense, has there been a more introspective writer than Thoreau. He watched his mind as a cat watches a mouse hole; and when the thought or feeling ventured forth, he pounced upon it with a skill born of long practice, and recorded it in his journal that night, and there it reposed, one more bit of real life won from chaos. He cared little, as I have said, for the factual world—events, even the largest, if they "transpired" outside his private universe, were insignificant. It did not occur to him that he might inhabit a double universe by bringing "the street" into his private universe and making fast friends of them. People in general committed the error of living in the street, and therefore, it seems, he would see what might be learned by living in his own "mind and heart." If he was not great enough to live wisely in both, he at least lived most thoroughly, most "intensively," in his chosen world. And this world was boundless. He was rarely introspective in the sense that he was solicitous of the welfare and the personal phenomena of Henry David Thoreau; when he looked within, it was to study spirit, soul, mind, the divinity in man. He was often quite indifferent as to Henry David Thoreau, in his absorption in the fragment of the general soul that chanced to dwell in that personality. Whoever can hold his faculties to this high enterprise may be called provincial or narrow in a most limited sense, for the self that is studied is essentially the self of everybody—the universal self....

Henry Seidel Canby

[On *Walden*]

The dominant idea of 'Walden,' which is simple, has been abundantly misunderstood. Thoreau's problem is the poor student's (or artist's or scientist's) who wishes to study, investigate, create, in a society which will not pay him enough for the proceeds of his labor, and is not interested in his brand of happiness. His

Reprinted from *Thoreau* (Boston: Houghton Mifflin Company, 1939), pp. 280–86, by permission of the publisher.

solution is self-reliance, simplification of living, willingness to labor with the hands if necessary, resignation of everything not essential to his particular temperament, and a shrewd study of how he can provide for his sustenance with the least waste of time. Thoreau's own estimate of time needed was a month to six weeks out of a year.

This solution is worthless, however, unless it brings with it an expansion of every taste, interest, vocation, and avocation which is possible to the experimenter, wished for by him, and practicable in a life of disciplined simplicity. 'Walden' calls for more life, not less. Nor is Thoreau's particular solution prescribed, like a reformer's panacea, to everyone, but only to the discontented who live lives of quiet desperation. 'Strong and valiant natures, who . . . spend more lavishly than the richest, without ever impoverishing themselves . . . those who are well employed,' can take care of themselves. He writes for that 'most terribly impoverished class of all, who have accumulated dross, but know not how to use it,' and 'the mass of men [alas, how much more numerous!] who are discontented, and idly complaining of . . . their lot or of the times, when they might improve them.' [1] 'I desire that there may be as many different persons in the world as possible; but I would have each one be very careful to find out and pursue *his own* way, and not his father's or his mother's or his neighbor's instead.' [2] The book is the story of how he, a poor scholar, and discontented, found *his way*, and how he enjoyed it.

The idea that 'Walden' is a study in asceticism is quite wrong. If Thoreau was an ascetic (though not always) in his eating, if he was an ascetic in physical love, nevertheless he was passionate in most of his pursuits, an epicure in many of the delights of the senses, and a propagandist for life that tingles from the brain to the toe-tips. He was unmarried and childless, which made his problem easier to solve economically, but no less a problem. Marriage—in a cabin with a bean or corn field—was raising poor whites all along the frontier, even as Thoreau wrote, and such simplicity solved no problems. If you wish to get married, if you love good wine, if you must live in a library, or go to Europe, or belong to a country club—these are merely the terms of your problem. The principle is the same—simplify in what is not necessary for your content. And if your needs are spiritual and intellectual, do not

---

[1] [*The Writings of Henry David Thoreau* (Boston, 1906)], II, 17, 18.
[2] *Idem*, 79.

starve them in order to feed less durable pleasures. Learn in any case what *you* can do in order to live the life you really desire while earning what you have to earn. Industrialism has made the problem of the man with a soul as well as a stomach more acute because it sells only for money, which must somehow be had. Thoreau's solution was to reduce his wants, grow beans for cash, build his house with his own hands, and be willing to be solitary as long and as much as solitude did him good. What is yours?

There were excellent reasons why 'Walden' was begun in the middle forties, put together in the late forties, and published in the early fifties.

The first reason for its writing I have already touched upon. Thoreau, in his Walden years, was outward bound; he had been forced to consider what society meant to him and what he meant to society. The challenge of 'Walden' was his answer.

But the more important reason was inwoven in the history of the country. The decade of the forties was a turning point in American social and moral development. The opening of the West, the rapid spread of railroads, most of all the development of the machine, had given the North and East—and New England particularly—a preponderance over the agrarian economy of the Southern planters. There was an extraordinary increase in production. New wealth and new wants grew. Texas land, California gold, and the Western trade were exploited all together in the same few years, and the railroads and the rapidly increasing merchant marine carried the new products to and from everywhere. Free—or nearly free—land became a new social factor. Settlements in fresh regions were now possible without the crushing hardships of earlier Western emigration. Labor, which had been turbulent, and whose problems Thoreau mentions more often than politics, was quieted by the drain to the frontiers. The cry, as the Beards say,[3] was changed from wages to ownership, perhaps by design. Socialism, so much in every thoughtful mind in the forties, was put off for generations.

Naturally, the intellectual and spiritual activities centering in New England were subtly affected by the vast if fluctuating increase in prosperity. The Concord intellectuals were optimists, even when they most deplored the uses made of prosperity. An Emerson in Carlyle's England, where industrialism was grinding the lower classes, is incredible. Thoreau in his 'Civil Disobedience' never so much as imagines an American state—or an American

---

[3] 'The Rise of American Civilization' (New York, 1928), *passim*.

economy—that would be forced to torture or to crush. His state is afraid of the citizens, afraid that they will escape without paying.

But the widespread speculation, the immense increase in material prosperity, which, in spite of the frequent panics, was characteristic of this fabulous age, was changing the moral mind of America. It was destroying quickly the ideals of conduct formed by the old ethics of damnation. It was producing no new ones, except the freedom, which became the duty, to get rich. There was a boom in New England in the very years when 'Walden' was being made into a book. Materialism spread, but what spread even faster was an intoxication of gain, a rapid expansion of the instincts for power, possession, sensual enjoyments. Genteel literature ignored this, but wherever the writer truly observes—whether a Mark Twain, or a recording journalist, or a letter writer, or a diarist—the facts show through. Historical fiction is feeding fat upon them today.

Against all of this Thoreau rebelled, as he naturally would. His bitter remarks on Australian and Californian gold are to be found in 'Life Without Principle,' and his comments on the intoxication of ownership everywhere in his writings. 'Walden' is a protest against his friend Horace Greeley's 'Go West, Young Man,' though it was not to the West itself but to the spirit in which men went there that he objected. His creed of simplicity is a protest against the get-rich-quick of free land and industrialism. Against land or industry he held no brief. But their exploiters who, he believed, were also self-exploiters to their hurt, were vigorous, successful, and also imaginative, real enemies, well worth fighting. The West, the machine, prosperity were all ideals—ideals captured by their greed.

The 'Week' had contained the literary and philosophic reflections of a youth sensitive to new thought but indifferent to his surroundings, except in so far as they were pregnant with the realities of nature or reminiscent of a past when men's experience, so he felt, came closer to a vital reality than in the streets and homes of Concord. 'Walden' was his recognition of a human present which he could no longer escape. It was a cockcrow (so he called it) to warn his neighbors that their souls were being enslaved. He wrote in terms of Concord farms and shops, not of manifest destiny in the West and the factories, but his near sight was clear sight. If he had gone West with Margaret Fuller he would never have written so truly, for, though she saw the degradation of morals and of morale, she, like Emerson, shared the intoxication of progress, and believed that these evils were transitory. 'Walden' is the story of a pioneer who stayed at home, who did not go bust in the panics, or get rich in the booms, who could, therefore, ask what this drunken prosperity would mean when all the railroad tracks were laid on Irishmen's bodies, when the emigrants were plowed into their own fields, and when the speculators, made rich by gambling, would have to ask, 'What next?'

The newly prosperous had their answer ready, and it was to become a slogan in the great days of expansion after the Civil War. They said, more land, more money, bigger cities, harder work, more power over nature; the future belongs to the millionaire, so let us all get rich together. Thoreau said, 'No.' 'When a man is warmed . . . what does he want next? Surely not more warmth of the same kind, as more and richer food, larger and more splendid houses, finer and more abundant clothing, more numerous, incessant, and hotter fires, and the like. When he has obtained those things which are necessary to life, there is another alternative than to obtain the superfluities; and that is, to adventure on life now, his vacation from humbler toil having commenced.' [4] He was wrong, of course. That was just what they were going to want, down to the last improvement in oil furnaces. The adventure in life which must not be deferred because living is so dear, was never to begin for the discontented mass of Americans trying to catch up with the Joneses, although some 'strong and valiant natures' would find abundant satisfactions in their competitions, being incapable of sucking anything else from the marrow of life. But more and more thoughtful and disillusioned Americans were to agree with Thoreau as the buoyant nineteenth century was merged in the dubious twentieth. 'Walden' had been, and remained, a tract for the times.

'Walden' was ready for publication in 1849. 'The Communist Manifesto' of Marx and Engels was published in 1848. There is no coincidence in this significant paralleling of dates. The same diseases of the profit system had impressed the American recluse and the German scholars. But three thousand miles and a philosophic abyss lay between Thoreau's solution in terms of morality and individualism, and the Communist rule of the proletariat. If Thoreau provided no technique by which society as a whole could escape from wage slavery, at least his challenge to Americans did not imply a dictatorship.

---

[4] [Thoreau], II, 16, 17.

F. O. Matthiessen

[The Organic Principle in *Walden*]

Wherever Thoreau turned for fresh confirmation of his belief that true beauty reveals necessity, he saw that 'Nature is a greater and more perfect art,' and that there is a similarity between her operations and man's even in the details and trifles. He held, like Emerson, that 'man's art has wisely imitated those forms into which all matter is most inclined to run, as foliage and fruit.' But Thoreau studied more examples in detail than Emerson did. Any glance from his door could provide him with fresh evidence. The sumach and pine and hickory that surrounded his cabin reminded him of the most graceful sculptural forms. The tracery of frostwork suggested the intricate refinements of design; and when he wanted his basic lesson in Coleridge's distinction between mechanic and organic form, all he had to do was to mould a handful of earth and to note that however separately interesting its particles might be, their relation was one of mere lifeless juxtaposition. In marked contrast was the shape of even 'the simplest and most lumpish fungus,' and the reasons for its fascination crowded upon him: 'it is so obviously organic and related to ourselves ... It is the expression of an idea; growth according to a law; matter not dormant, not raw, but inspired, appropriated by spirit.' With so many principles to be gleaned from the humblest growth, no wonder he held it 'monstrous when one cares but little about trees but much about Corinthian columns.'

When he tried to apply these principles to creation in literature, he sometimes was content with saying that 'true art is but the expression of our love of nature.' But he often pushed to a rigorous extreme not merely the supremacy of nature over art and of content over form, but also that of the artist's life over his work. He developed his own version of Milton's view that the heroic poem could be written only by the man who had lived a heroic life. As Thoreau put it, 'Nothing goes by luck in composition ... The best you can write will be the best that you are.' His distrust of 'the

Reprinted from *American Renaissance* (New York: Oxford University Press, 1941), pp. 154–56, 164–75, by permission of the publisher. Copyright 1941 by Oxford University Press, Inc.

belles lettres and the *beaux arts* and their professors' sprang from his desire to break down all artificial divisions between art and living. He often confronted the problem that 'it is not easy to write in a journal what interests us at any time, because to write it is not what interests us.' ¹ His only solution for this dilemma was, as he said in a letter to one of his followers: 'As for style of writing, if one has anything to say, it drops from him simply and directly, as a stone falls to the ground.' He came to the same point when he praised the style of John Brown: 'The *art* of composition is as simple as the discharge of a bullet from a rifle, and its masterpieces imply an infinitely greater force behind them. This unlettered man's speaking and writing are standard English. Some words and phrases deemed vulgarisms and Americanisms before, he has made standard American.' Again Thoreau was much closer than he knew to Greenough, who had insisted that the style indicated by our mechanics was miscalled economical and cheap. On the contrary, Greenough said, 'It is the dearest of styles . . . Its simplicity is not the simplicity of emptiness or of poverty, its simplicity is that of justness, I had almost said, of justice.'

When Thoreau said, 'Give me simple, cheap, and homely themes,' he had no notion that their execution would prove easy. Even when he declared that the real poem is what the poet himself has become, he added that 'our whole life is taxed for the least thing well done.' In adopting the tenet that poetry consists in knowing the quality of a thing, he had realized by his early thirties that such knowledge could be arrived at only through the slowest unconscious process, for 'at first blush a man is not capable of reporting truth; he must be drenched and saturated with it first. What was *enthusiasm* in the young man must become *temperament* in the mature man.' We might compare this with Lawrence's realization that 'we have to know ourselves pretty thoroughly before we can break through the automatism of ideals and conventions . . . Only through fine delicate knowledge can we recognize and release our impulses.' Only in seasoned maturity, to shift back to Thoreau's imagery, will the poet's truth exhale as naturally from him as 'the odor of the muskrat from the coat of the trapper.'

He often spoke of the organic style in an equally characteristic image—of its being a slow growth, unfolding under the care of the

---

¹ Or as he phrased it in an awkward couplet in the *Week:*

> My life has been the poem I would have writ,
> But I could not both live and utter it.

poet's patient hands. The degree to which his own practice lived
up to that metaphor is also the degree to which his craftsmanship
goes beyond Emerson's. He accepted the older man's view that
genius is the abundance of health, but was less intermittent in his
demand that talent must go with genius. To be sure, he hardly
ever discusses specific forms. He apparently took it for granted
that the artist's intuition will shape what is proper for it, and, in
the course of objecting to some of Carlyle's extravagances, said
little more than that the great writer works not by introducing new
forms but by reinvigorating old ones. However, in his perception
that this renewal comes through the fresh handling of words, he
generally sensed a more integral connection between the words
and the thought than Emerson did. That was why he regarded
translations as an impossibility, and held that the classics could be
read only after a training as rigorous 'as the athletes underwent.'
Moreover, he made another discrimination, essentially foreign to
Emerson, between the spoken and the written word. He held that
'what is called eloquence in the forum is commonly found to be
rhetoric in the study,' that however much we may admire the
orator's power, the style that lives beyond the emotion of the
moment demands a much more exacting composition. When Thoreau said of the poet, almost in Frost's words, that 'the tone and
pitch of his voice is the main thing,' he knew that 'a perfect expression requires a particular rhythm or measure for which no
other can be substituted.' Such knowledge—the product, as we
have seen, of his own sensitive organization—was his firmest
defense against the formlessness that beset his desire to speak in
harmony with nature. If it seldom rescued his immature verse—
almost the type instance of mechanic form in its imitation of the
surface tricks of the metaphysicals—it brought both precision and
timbre to the movement of his ripened prose. . . .

   In contrasting Thoreau with Emerson, Alcott felt that the former revealed secrets of nature 'older than fields and gardens,' that
'he seems alone, of all the men I have known, to be a native New
Englander.' Yet he could not help regretting at times that Thoreau
was so earthbound, and wished that he might come out of the
woods to the orchards, and so be pastoral instead of wild. It is
doubtful whether most readers now sense in Thoreau more than a
whiff of wildness. He wanted to bring into his writing 'muck from
the meadows'; but what he really managed to bring finds an apter

image in the delicate fragrance of the ferns or perhaps the ranker odor of the pines. His instinct towards the higher life was so inordinately encouraged by his contemporaries that it was only by the sturdiest action that he held fast to the soil. He described his most fertile process while saying why he went to the woods: 'Let us settle ourselves, and work and wedge our feet downward through the mud and slush of opinion, and prejudice, and tradition, and delusion, and appearance, that alluvion which covers the globe, through Paris and London, through New York and Boston and Concord, through Church and State, through poetry and philosophy and religion, till we come to a hard bottom and rocks in place, which we can call *reality*, and say, This is, and no mistake.'

This positive dredging beat reminds us again of his awareness of the physical basis of rhythm. It can remind us also of what Lawrence felt, that 'the promised land, if it be anywhere, lies away beneath our feet. No more prancing upwards. No more uplift.' Lawrence's discovery was quickened by watching and almost identifying himself with the downward thrust into the earth of the feet of Indian dancers. But Thoreau's knowledge was owing less directly to the Indians than to his re-creation for himself of the conditions of primitive life. He approximated Lawrence's words when he said that in good writing, 'the poem is drawn out from under the feet of the poet, his whole weight has rested on this ground.' Emerson, by contrast, wanted to 'walk upon the ground, but not to sink.' What Thoreau's language gained from his closer contact can be read in his evocation of a river walk, where every phrase is expressive of acute sensation: 'Now your feet expand on a smooth sandy bottom, now contract timidly on pebbles, now slump in genial fatty mud, amid the pads.'

But as you think again of the prolonged sensuous and rhythmical experience that Lawrence was able to make out of his response to the New Mexican corn dance, or of Hemingway's account of fishing on Big Two-Hearted River, you realize that Thoreau's product was ordinarily somewhat less full-bodied. When he said, 'Heaven is under our feet as well as over our heads,' he was speaking of the luminous clarity of the pond. A characteristic example to put beside Emerson's 'Snow-Storm' is the poem 'Smoke':

> Light-winged Smoke, Icarian bird,
> Melting thy pinions in thy upward flight,
> Lark without song, and messenger of dawn,
> Circling above the hamlets as thy nest;

> Or else, departing dream, and shadowy form
> Of midnight vision, gathering up thy skirts;
> By night star-veiling, and by day
> Darkening the light and blotting out the sun;
> Go thou my incense upward from this hearth,
> And ask the gods to pardon this clear flame.

The delicacy of the wraith-like movement finds its articulation in the succession of predominantly high-pitched vowels in the opening two lines. The 'Icarian bird,' a neat image for the melting away of the smoke in the bright morning sky, may then lead into too many fanciful conceits, but any tendency to vagueness is checked by the accurate epithet, 'star-veiling.' With that the contrast between the 'shadowy form' and the rays of light, latent from the start, flowers exquisitely and prepares the way for the final statement, which makes the poem no mere descriptive exercise but Thoreau's declaration of his ever fresh renewal of purpose with the kindling of his fire in the morning. The 'clear flame' of his spirit is so distinct and firm that it needs his plea for pardon to keep him from verging on *hubris* as he confidently contrasts his life with a world which is obscure and desperate in its confusion. That full contrast, to be sure, emerges only through the poem's context in *Walden*, but enough of the human situation is implied in the verses themselves to let them serve as a rounded, if minute, instance of Coleridge's distinction between imitation and mere copying. Coleridge held that the artist must not try to make a surface reproduction of nature's details, but 'must imitate that which is within the thing . . . for so only can he hope to produce any work truly natural in the object and truly human in the effect.' That combination has been created in this poem, since the reader's pleasure does not spring from the specific recordings, however accurate, but from the imperceptible interfusion with these of the author's own knowledge and feeling, and of his skill in evolving an appropriate form.

It is apparent, in view of this last distinction of Coleridge's, that the real test of whether Thoreau mastered organic form can hardly be made on the basis of accounting for the differences in body and flavor between his portrayal of the natural world and Emerson's, revelatory as these differences are. Nor can it be made by considering one of the rare occasions when his verse was redeemed by virtue of his discipline in translating from the Greek Anthology. Nor is it enough to reckon with the excellence of individual passages of prose, since the frequent charge is that whereas Emerson was master of the sentence, Thoreau was master of the paragraph, but that he was unable to go farther and attain 'the highest or structural achievements of form in a whole book.' The only adequate way of answering that is by considering the structure of *Walden* as a whole, by asking to what extent it meets Coleridge's demand of shaping, 'as it develops, itself from within.'

On one level *Walden* is the record of a personal experience, yet even in making that remark we are aware that this book does not go rightfully into the category of *Two Years Before the Mast* or *The Oregon Trail.* Why it presents a richer accumulation than either of those vigorous pieces of contemporary history is explained by its process of composition. Although Thoreau said that the bulk of its pages were written during his two years of sojourn by the pond (1845–7), it was not ready for publication until seven years later, and ultimately included a distillation from his journals over the whole period from 1838. A similar process had helped to transform his week's boat trip with his brother from a private to a symbolical event, since the record was bathed in memory for a decade (1839–49) before it found its final shape in words. But the flow of the *Week* is as leisurely and discursive as the bends in the Concord river, and the casual pouring in of miscellaneous poems and essays that Thoreau had previously printed in *The Dial* tends to obscure the cyclical movement. Yet each day advances from dawn to the varied sounds of night, and Thoreau uses an effective device for putting a period to the whole by the shift of the final morning from lazy August to the first sharp forebodings of transforming frost.

The sequence of *Walden* is arranged a good deal more subtly, perhaps because its subject constituted a more central symbol for Thoreau's accruing knowledge of life. He remarked on how the pond itself was one of the earliest scenes in his recollection, dating from the occasion when he had been brought out there one day when he was four, and how thereafter 'that woodland vision for a long time made the drapery of my dreams.' By 1841 he had already announced, 'I want to go soon and live away by the pond,' and when pressed by friends about what he would do when he got there, he had asked in turn if it would not be employment enough 'to watch the progress of the seasons'? In that same year he had said: 'I think I could write a poem to be called "Concord." For argument I should have the River, the Woods, the Ponds, the Hills, the Fields, the Swamps and Meadows, the Streets and Buildings, and the Villagers.' In his completed 'poem' these last elements had receded into the background. What had come squarely to the fore, and made the opening chapter by far the longest of all, was the desire to record an experiment in 'Economy' as an antidote to the 'lives of quiet desperation' that he saw the mass of men leading. This essay on how he solved his basic needs of food and shelter might stand by itself, but also carries naturally forward to the more poignant condensation of the same theme in 'Where I lived, and What I lived for,' which reaches its conclusion in the passage on wedging down to reality.

At this point the skill with which Thoreau evolved his composition begins to come into play. On the one hand, the treatment of his material might simply have followed the chronological outline; on the other, it might have drifted into being loosely topical. At first glance it may appear that the latter is what happened, that there is no real cogency in the order of the chapters. That would have been Lowell's complaint, that Thoreau 'had no artistic power such as controls a great work to the serene balance of completeness.' But so far as the opposite can be proved by the effective arrangement of his entire material, the firmness with which Thoreau binds his successive links is worth examining. The student and observer that he has settled himself to be at the end of his second chapter leads easily into his discussion of 'Reading,' but that in turn gives way to his concern with the more fundamental language, which all things speak, in the chapter on 'Sounds.' Then, after he has passed from the tantivy of wild pigeons to the whistle of the locomotive, he reflects that once the cars have gone by and the restless world with them, he is more alone than ever. That starts the transition to the chapter on 'Solitude,' in which the source of his joy is to live by himself in the midst of nature with his senses unimpaired. The natural contrast is made in the next chapter on 'Visitors,' which he opens by saying how he believes he loves society as much as most, and is ready enough to fasten himself 'like a bloodsucker for the time to any full-blooded man' who comes his way. But after he has talked enthusiastically about the French woodchopper, and other welcome friends from the village, he remembers 'restless committed men,' the self-styled reformers who felt it their duty to give him advice. At that he breaks away with 'Meanwhile my beans ... were impatient to be hoed'; and that opening carries him back to the earlier transition to the chapter on 'Sounds': 'I did not read books the first summer; I hoed beans.'

The effect of that repetition is to remind the reader of the time sequence that is knitting together all these chapters after the building of the cabin in the spring. From 'The Bean Field' as the sphere of his main occupation, he moves on, in 'The Village,' to his strolls for gossip, which, 'taken in homeopathic doses, was really as refreshing in its way as the rustle of leaves and the peeping of frogs.' Whether designedly or not, this chapter is the shortest in the book, and yields to rambles even farther away from the community than Walden, to 'The Ponds' and to fishing beyond 'Baker Farm.' As he was returning through the woods with his catch, and glimpsed in the near dark a woodchuck stealing across his path, then came the moment when he 'felt a strange thrill of savage delight, and was strongly tempted to seize and devour him raw.' And in the flash of his realization of his double instinct towards the spiritual and the wild, he has the starting point for the next two contrasting chapters, 'Higher Laws' and 'Brute Neighbors,' in considering both of which he follows his rule of going far enough to please his imagination.

From here on the structure becomes cyclical, his poem of the seasons or myth of the year. The accounts of his varied excursions have brought him to the day when he felt that he could no longer warm himself by the embers of the sun, which 'summer, like a departed hunter, had left.' Consequently he set about finishing his cabin by building a chimney, and called that act 'House-Warming.' There follows a solid block of winter in the three chapters, 'Winter Visitors,' 'Winter Animals,' and 'The Pond in Winter,' that order suggesting the way in which the radius of his experience contracted then more and more to his immediate surroundings. However, the last pages on the pond deal with the cutting of the ice, and end with that sudden extraordinary expansion of his thought which annihilates space and time.

The last movement is the advance to 'Spring.' The activity of the ice company in opening its large tracts has hastened the break-up of the rest of the pond; and, listening to its booming, he recalls that one attraction that brought him to the woods was the opportunity and leisure to watch this renewal of the world. He has long felt in his observations that a day is an epitome of a year, and now he knows that a year is likewise symbolical of a life; and so, in presenting his experience by the pond, he foreshortens and condenses the twenty-six months to the interval from the beginning of one summer to the next. In the melting season he feels more than ever the mood of expanding promise, and he catches the

reader up into this rich forward course by one of his most successful kinesthetic images, which serves to round out his cycle: 'And so
the seasons went rolling on into summer, as one rambles into higher
and higher grass.' To that he adds only the bare statement of when
he left the woods, and a 'Conclusion,' which explains that he did
so for as good a reason as he had gone there. He had other lives to
live, and he knew now that he could find for himself 'a solid
bottom everywhere.' That discovery gave him his final serene
assurance that 'There is more day to dawn,' and consequently he
was not to be disturbed by the 'confused *tintinnabulum*' that sometimes reached his midday repose. He recognized it for the noise of
his contemporaries.

The construction of the book involved deliberate rearrangement
of material. For instance, a single afternoon's return to the pond in
the fall of 1852 was capable of furnishing details that were woven
into half a dozen passages of the finished work, two of them sep-
arated by seventy pages. Nevertheless, since no invention was
demanded, since all the material was a *donnée* of Thoreau's
memory, my assertion that *Walden* does not belong with the simple
records of experience may require more establishing. The chief clue
to how it was transformed into something else lies in Thoreau's
extension of his remark that he did not believe himself to be 'wholly
involved in Nature.' He went on to say that in being aware of
himself as a human entity, he was 'sensible of a certain doubleness'
that made him both participant and spectator in any event. This
ability to stand 'as remote from myself as from another' is the in-
dispensable attribute of the dramatist. Thoreau makes you share
in the excitement of his private scenes, for example, by the kind
of generalized significance he can give to his purchase and de-
molishment of an old shanty for its boards:

> I was informed treacherously by a young Patrick that neighbor
> Seeley, an Irishman, in the intervals of the carting, transferred the
> still tolerable, straight, and drivable nails, staples, and spikes to
> his pocket, and then stood when I came back to pass the time of
> day, and look freshly up, unconcerned, with spring thoughts, at
> the devastation; there being a dearth of work, as he said. He was
> there to represent spectatordom, and help make this seemingly
> insignificant event one with the removal of the gods of Troy.

The demands he made of great books are significant of his own
intentions: 'They have no cause of their own to plead, but while
they enlighten and sustain the reader his common sense will not
refuse them.' Propaganda is not the source of the inner freedom

they offer to the reader, for their relation to life is more inclusive than argument; or, as Thoreau described it, they are at once 'intimate' and 'universal.' He aimed unerringly to reconcile these two extremes in his own writing. His experience had been fundamental in that it had sprung from his determination to start from obedience to the rudimentary needs of a man who wanted to be free. Greenough had seen how, in that sense, 'Obedience is worship,' for by discerning and following the functional patterns of daily behavior, you could discover the proportions of beauty that would express and complete them. It was Thoreau's conviction that by reducing life to its primitive conditions, he had come to the roots from which healthy art must flower, whether in Thessaly or Concord. It was not just a figure of speech when he said that 'Olympus is but the outside of the earth everywhere.' The light touch of his detachment allows the comparison of his small things with great, and throughout the book enables him to possess the universe at home.

As a result *Walden* has spoken to men of widely differing convictions, who have in common only the intensity of their devotion to life. It became a bible for many of the leaders of the British labor movement after Morris. When the sound of a little fountain in a shop window in Fleet Street made him think suddenly of lake water, Yeats remembered also his boyhood enthusiasm for Thoreau. He did not leave London then and go and live on Innisfree. But out of his loneliness in the foreign city he did write the first of his poems that met with a wide response, and 'The Lake Isle'—despite its Pre-Raphaelite flavor—was reminiscent of *Walden* even to 'the small cabin' Yeats built and the 'bean rows' he planted in his imagination. *Walden* was also one of our books that bulked largest for Tolstoy when he addressed his brief message to America (1901) and urged us to rediscover the greatness of our writers of the fifties: 'And I should like to ask the American people why they do not pay more attention to these voices (hardly to be replaced by those of financial and industrial millionaires, or successful generals and admirals), and continue the good work in which they made such hopeful progress.' In 1904 Proust wrote to the Comtesse de Noailles: 'Lisez ... les pages admirables de *Walden*. Il me semble qu'on les lise en soi-même tant elles sortent du fond de notre expérience intime.'

In his full utilization of his immediate resources Thoreau was the kind of native craftsman whom Greenough recognized as the harbinger of power for our arts. Craftsmanship in this sense involves the mastery of traditional modes and skills; it has been thought of more often in connection with Indian baskets or Yankee tankards and hearth-tools than with the so-called fine arts. In fact, until fairly lately, despite Greenough's pioneering, it has hardly been consistently thought of in relation to American products of any kind. The march of our experience has been so dominantly expansive, from one rapid disequilibrium to the next, that we have neglected to see what Constance Rourke, among others, has now pointed out so effectively: that notwithstanding the inevitable restlessness of our long era of pioneering, at many stages within that process the strong counter-effort of the settlers was for communal security and permanence. From such islands of realization and fulfilment within the onrushing torrent have come the objects, the order and balance of which now, when we most need them, we can recognize as among the most valuable possessions of our continent. The conspicuous manifestation of these qualities, as Greenough already knew, has been in architecture as the most social of forms, whether in the clipper, or on the New England green, or in the Shaker communities. But the artifacts of the cabinet maker, the potter and the founder, or whatever other utensils have been shaped patiently and devotedly for common service, are likewise a testimony of what Miss Rourke has called our classic art, recognizing that this term 'has nothing to do with grandeur, that it cannot be copied or imported, but is the outgrowth of a special mode of life and feeling.'

Thoreau's deep obligation to such traditional ways has been obscured by our thinking of him only as the extreme protestant. It is now clear that his revolt was bound up with a determination to do all he could to prevent the dignity of common labor from being degraded by the idle tastes of the rich. When he objected that 'the mason who finishes the cornice of the palace returns at night perchance to a hut not so good as a wigwam,' he showed the identity of his social and aesthetic foundations. Although he did not use Greenough's terms, he was always requiring a functional relationship. What he responded to as beauty was the application of trained skill to the exigencies of existence. He made no arbitrary separation between arts, and admired the Indian's woodcraft or the farmer's thorough care in building a barn on the same grounds that he admired the workmanship of Homer.[2] The depth to which his

---

[2] Emerson also said, 'I like a man who likes to see a fine barn as well as a good tragedy.' And Whitman added, as his reaction to the union of work and culture, 'I know that pleasure filters in and oozes out of me at the opera, but I know too that subtly and unaccountably my mind is sweet and odorous within while I clean up my boots and grease the pair that I reserve for stormy weather.'

ideals for fitness and beauty in writing were shaped, half unconsciously, by the modes of productive labor with which he was surrounded, or, in fact, by the work of his own hands in carpentry
or pencil-making or gardening, can be read in his instinctive analogies. He knew that the only discipline for Channing's 'sublimo-
slipshod style' would be to try to carve some truths as roundly and
solidly as a stonecutter. He knew it was no good to write, 'unless
you feel strong in the knees.' Or—a more unexpected example to
find in him—he believed he had learned an important lesson in
design from the fidelity with which the operative in the textile-
factory had woven his piece of cloth.

The structural wholeness of *Walden* makes it stand as the firmest product in our literature of such life-giving analogies between
the processes of art and daily work. Moreover, Thoreau's very lack
of invention brings him closer to the essential attributes of craftsmanship, if by that term we mean the strict, even spare, almost
impersonal 'revelation of the object,' in contrast to the 'elaborated
skill,' the combinations of more variegated resources that we
describe as technique. This contrast of terms is still Miss Rourke's,
in distinguishing between kinds of painting, but it can serve equally
to demonstrate why Thoreau's book possesses such solidity in contrast, say, with *Hiawatha* or *Evangeline*. Longfellow was much the
more obviously gifted in his available range of forms and subject
matters. But his graceful derivations from his models—the versifi-
cation and gentle tone of Goethe's *Hermann und Dorothea* for
Evangeline, or the metre of the *Kalevala* for *Hiawatha*—were not
brought into fusion with his native themes.[3] Any indigenous
strength was lessened by the reader's always being conscious of the
metrical dexterity as an ornamental exercise. It is certainly not to
be argued that technical proficiency must result in such dilutions,
but merely that, as Greenough saw, it was very hard for American
artists of that day, who had no developed tradition of their own,
not to be thus swamped by their contact with European influences.
Their very aspiration for higher standards of art than those with
which they were surrounded tended to make them think of form
as a decorative refinement which could be imported.

The particular value of the organic principle for a provincial
society thus comes into full relief. Thoreau's literal acceptance of
Emerson's proposition that vital form 'is only discovered and exe-

---

[3] And as F. L. Pattee has said of *Hiawatha,* in *The Feminine Fifties* (1940):
'The only really Indian thing about the poem is the Indian summer haze
that softens all its outlines, but even this atmosphere is Indian only in name:
it was borrowed from German romantic poets.'

cuted by the artist, not arbitrarily composed by him,' impelled him to minute inspection of his own existence and of the intuitions that rose from it. Although this involved the restriction of his art to parochial limits, to the portrayal of man in terms only of the immediate nature that drew him out, his study of this interaction also brought him to fundamental human patterns unsuspected by Longfellow. Thoreau demonstrated what Emerson had merely observed, that the function of the artist in society is always to renew the primitive experience of the race, that he 'still goes back for materials and begins again on the most advanced stage.' Thoreau's scent for wildness ferreted beneath the merely conscious levels of cultivated man. It served him, in several pages of notes about a debauched muskrat hunter (1859), to uncover and unite once more the chief sources for his own art. He had found himself heartened by the seemingly inexhaustible vitality of this battered character, 'not despairing of life, but keeping the same rank and savage hold on it that his predecessors have for so many generations, while so many are sick and despairing.' Thoreau went on, therefore, half-playfully to speculate what it was that made this man become excited, indeed inspired by the January freshet in the meadows:

> There are poets of all kinds and degrees, little known to each other. The Lake School is not the only or the principal one. They love various things. Some love beauty, and some love rum. Some go to Rome, and some go a-fishing, and are sent to the house of correction once a month ... I meet these gods of the river and woods with sparkling faces (like Apollo's) late from the house of correction, it may be carrying whatever mystic and forbidden bottles or other vessels concealed, while the dull regular priests are steering their parish rafts in a prose mood. What care I to see galleries full of representatives of heathen gods, when I can see natural living ones by an infinitely superior artist, without perspective tube? If you read the Rig Veda, oldest of books, as it were, describing a very primitive people and condition of things, you hear in their prayers of a still older, more primitive and aboriginal race in their midst and round about, warring on them and seizing their flocks and herds, infesting their pastures. Thus is it in another sense in all communities, and hence the prisons and police.

The meandering course of Thoreau's reflections here should not obscure his full discovery that the uneradicated wildness of man is the anarchical basis both of all that is most dangerous and most valuable in him. That he could dig down to the roots of primitive poetry without going a mile from Concord accounts for his ability to create 'a true Homeric or Paphlagonian man' in the likeness of the French woodchopper. It also helps account for the fact that by following to its uncompromising conclusion his belief that great art can grow from the center of the simplest life, he was able to be universal. He had understood that in the act of expression a man's whole being, and his natural and social background as well, function organically together. He had mastered a definition of art akin to what Maritain has extracted from scholasticism: *Recta ratio factibilium*, the right ordering of the thing to be made, the right revelation of the material.

Joseph Wood Krutch

Paradise Found

A Week on the Concord and Merrimack Rivers had been the account of a vacation, which is to say of an interlude, a truancy, or an escape. *Walden* was an account of a way of life, even of a permanent way of life if one considers that what it describes is not merely a way of living by a pond but a general attitude capable of making life so simple that there is, as Thoreau put it, no need for the brow to sweat. The finder can be, as the seeker seldom is, gay; and *Walden* is, among many other things, a gay book. In the *Journal* Thoreau speaks often of joy and even of ecstasy. He may at most periods of his life have known a good deal of both, although it is also evident that he had moments, especially as he grew older, when the transcendental voices remained stubbornly silent and even nature awoke only feeble response. But neither joy nor ecstasy is the same as gaiety, and in *Walden* there is much that can hardly be called by any other name. He is gay when he describes the routine of daily living, gay when he reports his interviews with

Reprinted from *Henry David Thoreau* (New York: William Sloane Associates, Inc., 1948), pp. 105–14, by permission of William Morrow and Company, Inc. Copyright 1948 by William Sloane Associates, Inc.

visitors human or animal, and gay when he flings into the face of his fellow citizens his account of their preposterous, self-imposed labors—Herculean in their magnitude, Sisyphean in their endless futility. And he is gayest of all, perhaps, when he goads them with some blasphemy, some gently insinuated renunciation of stern duty. . . .

. . . [There] are four related but distinct "matters" with which the book concerns itself, and they might be enumerated as follows: (1) The life of quiet desperation which most men lead. (2) The economic fallacy which is responsible for the situation in which they find themselves. (3) What the life close to nature is and what rewards it offers. (4) The "higher laws" which man begins, through some transcendental process, to perceive if he faithfully climbs the stepladder of nature whose first rung is "wildness," whose second is some such gentle and austere but not artificial life as Thoreau himself was leading, and whose third is the transcendental insight he only occasionally reached.

The elements of an inclusive system are present, scattered here and there through the logically (though not artistically) fragmentary discourse. Thoreau has, for instance, a theory of wages and costs ("the cost of a thing is the amount of what I will call life which is required to be exchanged for it, immediately or in the long run") and a somewhat Marxian—and Carlylesque—conception of production for use ("I cannot believe that our factory system is the best mode by which men get clothing . . . since, as far as I have heard or observed, the principal object is, not that mankind may be well and honestly clad, but, unquestionably, that the corporations may be enriched"). He has also, however, a theory of ultimate value which is metaphysical rather than economic. That theory of ultimate value, together with the distrust of mass action which goes with it, leads him away from any concern with social reforms other than those which every man can achieve for himself. It also leads him in the direction of a solitary life in nature to which he was temperamentally inclined and which can be justified on mystical grounds. It is a bridge across which he may go toward those ultimate ends the Transcendentalists and the wise Orientals are seeking.

The fact that he never attempts to schematize these various convictions has, moreover, the effect of making *Walden* more persuasive, or at least more difficult to controvert, than would otherwise be the case, because it makes it less easy for the reader to get hold of any link in a chain of reasoning which he is tempted to

try to break. Thoreau does not so much argue that it is possible
and desirable to live in a certain way as tell us how he lived and
what rewards he discovered. He presents us, as it were, with a *fait
accompli*, and, like Captain Shotover in Shaw's *Heartbreak House*,
he will not abide our question. He discharges a shaft, and is gone
again before we can object or challenge.

For all his seeming directness he is extremely difficult to corner.
No writer was ever, at dangerous moments, more elusive, and no
proponent of fundamental paradoxes ever more skillfully provided
himself with avenues of escape. His residence at Walden is, when
he wishes to make it so, an experiment whose results have universal
significance; but it can, on convenient occasion, shrink to the status
of a merely personal expedient. It is alternately, as a point is to be
made or an objection to be met, a universal nostrum or the whim
of an individual eccentric. In the second paragraph he pretends
that he writes the account only because his neighbors have expressed curiosity concerning such matters as are implied in their
questions concerning what he got to eat and whether or not he
felt lonesome. He will, he says, talk principally about himself because there is no one else whom he knows so well. But the very
next paragraph begins: "I would fain say something . . . concerning . . . you who read these pages, who are said to live in New
England; something about your condition . . . in this world, in this
town, what it is, whether it is necessary that it be as bad as it is,
whether it cannot be improved as well as not." And he is off for
many pages which are not about himself or how he lived at Walden,
but about how others live elsewhere. He did not come into the
world, he had previously protested, to make it better; and yet,
until you catch him at it, this is exactly what he is trying to do.
When you do catch him at it, he retreats again into the extremest
possible individualism. In some sense he is certainly suggesting
that others imitate him; but he also protests that he would like
to have as many different kinds of men in the world as possible. If
you ask him what would happen if all tried to find a pond to live
beside, he answers that he never suggested they should; that in
fact he himself lived there for only two years; and that he left,
perhaps, because he had some other lives to lead.

. . . Thoreau makes, if you like, a foray into sociology, but it is a
raid, not a plan of conquest, and its aim is to harass and disturb
the enemy—not to impose the will of a benevolent conqueror upon
it. The impregnable fortress into which he retreats is the fortress
of absolute individualism, the declaration that he is not responsible

for anything except his own soul. "I, on my side, require of every writer, first or last, a simple and sincere account of his own life . . . some such account as he would send to his kindred from a distant land; for if he has lived sincerely, it must have been in a distant land to me." Nonconformity and uniqueness are the ideals. "If a man does not keep pace with his companions, perhaps it is because he hears a different drummer. Let him step to the music which he hears, however measured or far away." The very most he can pretend ultimately to teach by being himself is that other men should also be themselves. . . .

Thoreau's cabin at Walden has already been likened to the poet's symbolical garret, to Robinson Crusoe's island, and to a one-man Brook Farm. It was also Diogenes' tub and, during the philosopher's moments of asceticism, St. Simeon's pillar. Like each of these it helped dramatize a personality and from each at least one chapter of the book might appropriately have been dated. Nor is it meaningful to ask in which the real Thoreau dwelt. The real Thoreau was to some extent at home in all of them though he dwelt no more steadily in any than he did on his Crusoe's island.

The original Robinson was a solitary by force of circumstances and not at all by choice. Ostensibly his adventure was not an adventure but a misfortune, and, at face value, the book which describes his singlehanded conquest of nature ought to be read with the most sympathy by philosophical cockneys. But, if we are right in assuming that making Crusoe so unappreciative of the meaning of his predicament is only a shrewd literary device and that he is remembered because his adventure translates into realistic terms the old daydream of life in the golden age when nature sufficed to satisfy all man's needs without the intervention of any social machinery, then Crusoeism is not too inappropriate a name to serve for that part of the Walden experiment, and for those sections of *Walden*, the book, which are not concerned either with unmistakably Transcendental notions or explicit social lessons. Such Crusoeism was certainly the thing that Thoreau first became aware of in himself, and the most nearly unique part of his writing is that which describes the ecstasies and contentments of a life which he felt was as little dependent upon any resources other than his own and nature's as Robinson's ever was, and in the leading of which he accepted the few manufactured articles which he used as casually and as uncritically as Robinson took those that were washed ashore or fetched from the wreck. Thoreau the "nature writer" seems to owe less to any predecessors than Thoreau the mystic owes to Emerson and others, or than Thoreau the economist owes to Carlyle and, directly or indirectly, to the other radicals who were inspiring all New England to Utopian experiments. But if it is the Transcendentalist who is most often discussed by literary historians and the social protestant who is most often cited with respect by the leaders in world affairs, it is probably the Thoreau who turns his back upon mankind who has the most devoted readers. Probably he has sent more men into the woods (though few have actually lived as he did) than into either asceticism on the one hand, or political activity on the other.

One of the most important aspects of *Walden* as a classic must, then, be its success as a work of the imagination rather than as a work of moral or social criticism. That many of its ideas were seminal may turn out to be, ultimately, the most significant thing about it, but its apparently ever-increasing popularity with readers who cherish it as a precious and sometimes almost secret possession is probably due principally to the fact that it has become a locus for the presentation of certain emotional attitudes, the classic record of one kind of life and one kind of sensibility, just as, let us say, the *Confessions* of Rousseau became the classic account of a different kind of life and a different set of sensibilities. Many men have found themselves, or some dream of themselves, in his pages. Pilgrimages are made to Concord in the same way—and for the same reasons—that they are made to Stoke Poges or to Assisi.

None of this would have been possible if Thoreau had not lived at Walden or rather if he had not seized upon and dramatized the fact. If, for instance, all the leading themes of his masterpiece had been expounded equally well in his earlier book, that book could never have achieved equal acceptance for the simple reason that a man cannot be remembered for having spent a week on a river as he can be remembered in association with a place— especially with a place as well named as Thoreau's pond was. His act, or at least his dramatization of it, was a stroke of the creative imagination and so successful that Thoreau is the man who lived at Walden in somewhat the same way that Dante was the man who visited Hell. And the fact that the adventure was in itself so unspectacular is but another aspect of perfect artistic appropriateness because it emphasized so dramatically one of the points which he wished to make. Let others seek the North Pole or the sources of the Nile. Walden is just as far away if measured in terms of the only distance that counts. It is an Ultima Thule which no man can say that he is prevented by any circumstances from visiting.

Sherman Paul

Resolution at Walden

I

Walden was published in 1854, eight years before Thoreau died, some seven years after his life in the woods. His journal shows that he had proposed such a "poem" for himself as early as 1841, that its argument would be "the River, the Woods, the Ponds, the Hills, the Fields, the Swamps and Meadows, the Streets and Buildings, and the Villagers. Then Morning, Noon, and Evening, Spring, Summer, Autumn, and Winter, Night, Indian Summer, and the Mountains in the Horizon." Like *A Week on the Concord and Merrimack Rivers* (1849) — "If one would reflect," Thoreau had written in 1837, "let him embark on some placid stream, and float with the current" — *Walden* took a long time maturing, a longer time, because it was more than the stream of his reflections. The *Week* had been written out of joyousness and to memorialize his most perfect excursion in nature. *Walden*, however, was Thoreau's recollected experience, recollected not in tranquillity, but in the years of what he himself called his "decay." Although one need only search the journals to find many of the events of *Walden* freshly put down, *Walden* itself reveals that Thoreau was now looking at these events with more experienced eyes: his long quarrel with society has intervened, his youthful inspiration had become more difficult to summon, the harvest of the *Week* he had hoped to bestow on the public lay in his attic, and, growing older, he was still without a vocation that others would recognize. In *Walden*, at once his victorious hymn to Nature, to her perpetual forces of life, inspiration and renewal, Thoreau defended his vocation by creating its eternal symbol.

The common moral of *Walden* is that of the virtue of simplicity; and simplicity is usually taken on the prudential level of economy with which Thoreau seemingly began the book. In terms of Thoreau's spiritual economy, however, simplicity was more than freedom from the burdens of a mortgaged life: it was an ascetic, a severe dicipline, like solitude for Emerson, by which Thoreau concentrated his forces and was able to confront the facts of life

Reprinted from *Accent,* XIII (Spring 1953), 101–13, by permission of the author and the University of Illinois Foundation.

without the intervening barriers of society or possessions. For simplicity, Thoreau often substituted poverty, a word which both set him apart from his materialistic neighbors and hallowed his vocation with its religious associations of renunciation and higher dedication. It was the suitable condition for the spiritual crusader: the sign in a land of traders of his profession. But it also signified his inner condition. "By poverty," he said, "*i.e.* simplicity of life and fewness of incidents, I am solidified and crystallized, as a vapor or liquid by cold. It is a singular concentration of strength and energy and flavor. Chastity is perpetual acquaintance with the All. My diffuse and vaporous life becomes as frost leaves and spiculae radiant as gems on the weeds and stubble in a winter morning." Such poverty or purity was a necessity of *his* economy. "You think," he continued, "that I am impoverishing myself by withdrawing from men, but in my solitude I have woven for myself a silken web or *chrysalis*, and, nymph-like, shall ere long burst forth a more perfect creature, fitted for a higher society. By simplicity, commonly called poverty, my life is concentrated and so becomes organized, or a κόσμος, which before was inorganic and lumpish."

This was also the hope of his paean to spring in *Walden*, to "pass from the lumpish grub in the earth to the airy and fluttering butterfly." The purpose of his experiment at Walden Pond, begun near the end of his years of undisciplined rapture—Emerson said that the vital heat of the poet begins to ebb at thirty—was to build an organic life as consciously as he built his hut (and his book), and so retain his vital heat. "May I never," he had recorded in his journal, "let the vestal fire go out in my recesses." But there was desperation in his attempt to keep his vital heat, because it was only *vital* (or rather he felt it so) when he was maturing beyond the lumpish, grub-like existence. As well as the advocacy of the organic life which promised renewal and growth, *Walden* for Thoreau filled the immediate need of self-therapy. In the serenity and joy of his art this is often overlooked, but it is there in the journals behind the book. And the greatness of *Walden*, from this perspective at least, is the resolution Thoreau was able to fulfill through art. By creating an organic form he effected his own resolution for rebirth: by conscious endeavor he recaptured, if not the youthful ecstasy of his golden age, a mature serenity.

This serenity, however, is still alert, wakeful, tense. It was a victory of discipline. "That aim in life is highest," Thoreau noted during the composition of *Walden*, "which requires the highest

and finest discipline." That aim was highest, that discipline the
highest vocation, because the goal and fulfillment of all transcendental callings was purity—a oneness with Nature in which the
untarnished mirror of the soul reflected the fullness of being. The
cost of doing without conventional life was not too great for
Thoreau, considering his desire to "perceive things truly and
simply." He believed that "a fatal coarseness is the result of mixing
in the trivial affairs of men." And to justify his devotion to purity
he wrote *Walden,* a promise of the higher society a man can make
when he finds his *natural* center, a record of things and events so
simple and fundamental that all lives less courageous and prin-
cipled are shamed by the *realometer* it provides. Like other master-
works of its time, it has the unique strain of American romanticism: behind its insistent individualism and desire for experience,
there is still more earnest conviction of the necessity of virtue.

II

In the concluding pages of *Walden,* Thoreau remarked that "in
this part of the world it is considered a ground for complaint if a
man's writings admit of more than one interpretation." With his
contemporaries, Emerson, Hawthorne, Melville, he wanted the
"volatile truth" of his words to "betray the inadequacy of the
residual statement." He would have considered *Walden* a failure
if it served only to communicate an eccentric's refusal to go along
with society, if, taken literally, its spiritual courage was thinned
to pap for tired businessmen long since beyond the point of no
return. For *Walden* was *his* myth: "A fact truly and absolutely
stated," he said, "is taken out of the region of common sense and
acquires a mythologic or universal significance." This was the
extravagance he sought—this going beyond the bounds. For him,
only the fact stated without reference to convention or institution,
with only reference to the self which has tasted the world and
digested it, which has been "drenched" and "saturated" with
truth, is properly humanized—is properly myth. Primarily to im-
merse himself in truth, to merge himself with the law of Nature,
and to humanize this experience by the alchemy of language,
Thoreau went to Walden. There, free from external references,
he could purify himself and live a sympathetic existence, alive to
the currents of being. What he reported, then, would be the experience of the self in its unfolding and exploration of the "not-
me." The literal record would merely remain the residual state-

ment—no one knew better the need for concrete fact; but it would also yield a *translated* meaning.

The whole of *Walden* is an experience of the microcosmic and cosmic travels of the self. At Walden Pond, Thoreau wrote, "I have, as it were, my own sun and moon and stars, and a little world all to myself." Thoreau, of course, was a great traveller, if only a saunterer. The profession of traveller appealed to his imagination; it was, he said, the "best symbol of our life." And "Walking" was the best short statement of his way of life, of his journey to the holy land. He yearned, he wrote in 1851, "for one of those old, meandering, dry, uninhabited roads, which lead away from towns. . . ." He wanted to find a place "where you can walk and think with least obstruction, there being nothing to measure progress by; where you can pace when your breast is full, and cherish your moodiness; where you are not in false relations with men. . . ." He wanted "a road where I can travel," where "I can walk, and recover the lost child that I am without any ringing of a bell." The road he wanted led to Walden. There he regained the primal world, and lived the pristine initiation into consciousness over again. "Both place and time were changed," he said in *Walden*, "and I dwelt nearer to those parts of the universe and to those eras in history which had most attracted me."

In this effort to live out of time and space or to live in all times and places, *Walden* immediately suggests Melville's *Moby-Dick*. Melville had written another voyage of the self on which he explored reality, charted the constituents of a chaos, and raised his discovery to the universal level of archetypal experience. He had elaborated the myth of the hunter which Thoreau also employed in the chapter on "Higher Laws." "There is a period in the history of the individual, as of the race," he wrote, "when hunters are the 'best men'. . . ." Hunting, he added, "is oftenest the young man's introduction to the forest [Melville's sea], and the most original part of himself. He goes thither at first as a hunter and fisher, until at last, if he has the seeds of a better life in him, he distinguishes his proper objects. . . ." It was in these "wild" employments of his youth that Thoreau acknowledged his "closest acquaintance with Nature." For Nature revealed herself to the hunter more readily than to "philosophers or poets even, who approach her with expectation"—or, as Melville knew, to the participant and not the observer of life. If Thoreau had long since given up hunting, he still found a sustaining link with the wild in his bean field.

There are obvious differences, of course, in the quality of these travels — each author had his spiritual torment, Melville the need for belief, Thoreau the need for recommunion. But both were projecting the drama of their selves, a drama that in both instances ended in rebirth; and the methods both employed were remarkably similar. Each abstracted himself from the conventional world, established a microcosm by which to test the conventions, and worked at a basic and heroic occupation. For example, the village stands in the same symbolic relation to Thoreau at Walden that the land does to Melville's sea; and it is the occupation in both that supplies the residual statement. In Thoreau's case, it is also a primitive concern with essentials: building his hut, planting, hoeing and harvesting his beans, fishing and naturalizing. And the nature of the occupation gives each its spiritual quality, because whaling (butchery) and colonizing (building from scratch) are projections of different visions of the universe of which only the central similarity remains—the exploration of self.

But this similarity is a sufficient signature for both; one recognizes the existential kinship. At the conclusion of *Walden* Thoreau declared: "Explore thyself . . . Be . . . the Mungo Park, the Lewis and Clark and Frobisher, of your own streams and oceans. . . ."—

> ". . . . . be
> Expert in home-cosmography."

For "there are continents and seas in the moral world to which every man is an isthmus or an inlet, yet unexplored by him, . . . [and] it is easier to sail many thousand miles through cold and storm and cannibals, in a government ship, with five hundred men and boys to assist one, than it is to explore the private sea, the Atlantic and Pacific Ocean of one's being alone." Melville at Pittsfield would have agreed that "herein are demanded the eye and the nerve." But if Melville needed the watery two-thirds of the world and the great whale for this quest, Thoreau, who had the gift of enlarging the small, needed only the pond and its pickerel. And where Melville needed the destructive forces of the sea to mirror himself, Thoreau, who had seen the place of violence in the total economy of nature, needed only the recurrence of the seasons.

III

Walden was Thoreau's quest for a reality he had lost, and for this reason it was a quest for purity. Purity meant a return to the spring (and springtime) of life, to the golden age of his youth and active senses, when the mirror of his self was not clouded by self-consciousness. *Walden*, accordingly, follows the cycle of developing consciousness, a cycle that parallels the change of the seasons. It is a recapitulation of Thoreau's development (and the artistic reason he put the experience of two years into one)—a development from the sensuous, active, external (unconscious *and* out-of-doors) summer of life through the stages of autumnal consciousness and the withdrawal inward to the self-reflection of winter, to the promise of ecstatic rebirth in the spring. It was a matter of purification because Thoreau had reached the winter of decay at the time *Walden* was being revised for the press. With consciousness had come the knowledge of the "reptile" and "sensual" which he knew could not "be wholly expelled." "I fear," he wrote, "that it [the sensual] may enjoy a certain health of its own; that we may be well, yet not pure." For the mind's approach to God, he knew that the severest discipline was necessary; his chapter on "Higher Laws" is concerned almost entirely with the regimen of the appetites because "man flows at once to God when the channel of purity is open." The undeniable sensual energy— the "generative energy"—he had unconsciously enjoyed in the ecstasy of youth, now needed control. "The generative energy," he wrote, "which, when we are loose, dissipates and makes us unclean, when we are continent invigorates and inspires us." He was consciously using instinct for higher ends, seeking chastity by control.

In Walden Pond he saw the image of his purified self—that pristine, eternal self he hoped to possess. In 1853, while he was working on his book, he noted in his journal: "How watchful we must be to keep the crystal well that we were made, clear!—that it be not made turbid by our contact with the world, so that it will not reflect objects." The pond, he recalled, was one of the "oldest scenes stamped on my memory." He had been taken to see it when he was four years old. Now, playing his flute beside its waters, his beans, corn and potatoes replacing the damage of the years, he felt that another aspect was being prepared "for new infant eyes," that "even I have at length helped to clothe that fabulous landscape of my infant dreams...." Later, he recalled his youthful reveries on its waters: "I have spent many an hour, when I was younger, floating over its surface as the zephyr willed ... dreaming awake...." But time (and woodchoppers) had ravished its shores: "My Muse may be excused," he explained, "if she is silent henceforth. How can you expect the birds to sing when their groves are cut down?" It was the confession of the Apollo who had had to serve Admetus, a confession he made again in "Walking." Visited by fewer thoughts each year, he said that "the grove in our minds is laid waste—sold to feed unnecessary fires of ambition. . . ."

But Thoreau discovered at Walden that even though the groves were cut down, the pond itself remained the same—it "best preserves its purity." "It is itself unchanged," he learns, "the same water my youthful eyes fell on; all the change is in me. . . . It is perennially young. . . ." Catching sight of his eternal self and realizing that the waste of years had only touched his shore, his empirical self, he exclaimed, "Why, here is Walden, the same woodland lake that I discovered so many years ago . . . it is the same liquid joy and happiness to itself and its Maker, ay, and it *may* be to me." The pond, so constant, clear and pure, was truly the *Walled in* pond, the undefiled soul of which the Thoreau-in-decay said, "I am its stony shore. . . ."

If Thoreau spent his youth drifting with the inspiring zephyrs on Walden's surface, he now plumbed its depths, angled for its pickerel and its bottom. For it was the purpose of *Walden* to find bottom, to affirm reality; and the reality Thoreau discovered in the soul and in the whole economy of Nature he found at the bottom of the pond. What renewed his faith was the sign of the never-dying, all-promising generative force which he symbolized when he wrote: ". . . a bright green weed is brought up on anchors even in midwinter." The hope of a renewed life, rhapsodized in the concluding chapters of *Walden* and there symbolized in the hardy blade of grass—the green flame of life—, was the assurance he now had that "there is nothing inorganic."

And by sounding the bottom Thoreau also discovered the law of the universe and of the intellect that made possible his organic participation in the process of renewal and provided him the guarantee of its expression in natural objects. "The regularity of the bottom and its conformity to the shores and the range of the neighboring hills were so perfect," he wrote, "that a distant promontory betrayed itself in the soundings quite across the pond, and its direction could be determined by observing the opposite shore." He found, too, that the intersection of the lines of greatest length and breadth coincided with the point of greatest depth; and he suggested that this physical law might be applied to ethics. "Draw lines through the length and breadth of the aggregate of a man's particular daily behaviors and waves of life into his coves and inlets, and where they intersect will be the height or depth of his character. Perhaps we need only to know how his shores tend and his adjacent country or circumstances, to infer his depth and concealed bottom." *Walden* was just such an account of Thoreau's moral topography, and if the lines were drawn, the pond itself would be his center. For wasn't the eternal self, like the pond, " 'God's Drop' "?

The search for the bottom was conscious exploration. Here, and in the passages on fishing for pickerel and chasing the loon, Thoreau was not a naturalist but a natural historian of the intellect, using the natural facts as symbols for his quest for inspiration and thought. In "Brute Neighbors" he had asked, "Why do precisely these objects which we behold make a world?" And he had answered that "they are all beasts of burden . . . made to carry some portion of our thoughts." The natural world merely reflects ourselves. Having overcome his doubts of this central article of transcendental faith by assuring himself of the regularity of Walden's depth—that the hidden reality corresponded to its visible shores, that "Heaven is under our feet as well as over our heads"—he could trust once more his own projection of mood and thought to be reflected in its proper and corresponding object. He had noted in his journal that the poet "sees a flower or other object, and it is beautiful or affecting to him because it is a symbol of his thought, and what he indistinctly feels or perceives is matured in some other organization. The objects I behold correspond to my mood." His concern with the pond and the seasons, then, was symbolic of his soul's preoccupation. "Our moulting season . . . must be the crisis in our lives," he said; and like the loon he retired to a solitary pond to spend it. There, like the caterpillar—to use another symbol—, "by an internal industry and expansion" he cast off his "wormy coat."

IV

Thoreau went to Walden to become an unaccommodated man, to shed his lendings and to find his naked and sufficient self. Of this, the pond was the symbol. He also went to clothe himself in response to his inner needs. Building an organic life was again a conscious endeavor which was chastened by the necessity of maintaining his vital heat—the heat of body and spirit; for his purpose was not to return to nature, but to combine "the hardiness of . . . savages with the intellectualness of the civilized man." "The civilized man," he said, "is a more experienced and wiser savage," meaning, of course, that the instinctive life was most rewarding when channeled by intellectual principles. "What was *enthusiasm* in the young man," he wrote during the crisis of his life, "must become *temperament* in the mature man." The woodchopper, the animal man, must be educated to consciousness, and still retain his innocence. Properly seen in the total economy of Nature the once freely taken gift of inspiration must be earned by perceiving the law of Nature, by the tragic awareness that inspiration, like its source, has its seasons. The villagers, Thoreau wrote indignantly, "instead of going to the pond to bathe or drink, are thinking to bring its waters, which should be as sacred as the Ganges at least, to the village in a pipe, to wash their dishes with!—to earn their Walden by the turning of a cock or drawing of a plug!" The spiritual soldier had learned that after laying siege to Nature, only passivity would bring victory.

Thoreau earned his Walden by awaiting the return of spring, by sharing the organic process. Of this his hut and his bean-field became the symbols. The latter, as we have seen, helped to renew the aspect of the pond; as the work of the active self, it was rightly an alteration of the shore. And the pond, as the pure, eternal self —the "perfect forest mirror"—, was the calm surface on which these purifying activities were reflected. Thoreau labored in his bean-field because he took seriously Emerson's injunction to action in *The American Scholar*. He knew that the higher ends of the activity of the empirical self were self-consciousness, that the eternal self, the passive center, only acquired consciousness by observing the empirical self at work on the circumference. He recognized "a certain doubleness by which I can stand as remote from myself as from another." "However intense my experience," he wrote, "I am conscious of the presence of and criticism of a part of me, which, as it were, is not part of me, but spectator, sharing no experience, but taking note of it. . . ." The reward of activity, the result of this drama of selves, was self-reflection, insight. "All perception of truth is the detection of an analogy," Thoreau noted in the journal; "we reason from our hands to our head." And so through the labor of the hands, even to the point of drudgery, he was "determined to know beans." He did not need the beans for food but for sympathy with Nature; he needed to work them because, as he said, "They attached me to the earth, and so I got strength like Antaeus." His fields were also symbolic of his attempt to link the wild and the cultivated. And the "immeasurable crop" his devoted hoeing yielded came from the penetration of the earth's crust—a knowledge of the depths similar in significance to Melville's descent to the unwarped primal world. "I disturbed," Thoreau wrote, "the ashes of unchronicled nations who in primeval times lived under these heavens. . . ." In his bean-field beside Walden he was not serving Admetus, for he had found a way to delve beneath the "established order on the surface."

The prudential value of this labor came to $16.94, but the spiritual value was the realization that the Massachusetts soil could sustain the seeds of virtue—that in Thoreau's case at least, the seed had not lost its vitality and that the harvest of his example might be "a new generation of men." Later on, in the chapter on "Former Inhabitants," he again disturbed the surface by delving into the past, comparing his life at Walden to the defeated lives of its previous occupants. Here, Thoreau expressed his desire for the higher society, the ideal community in which he could wholly participate and which he hoped he was beginning. "Again, perhaps, Nature will try," he wrote, "with me for the first settler. . . . I am not aware that any man has ever built on the spot which I occupy." Like Joyce's Finnegan, he was to be the father of cities, not those reared on ancient sites, but cities growing out of the union with the earth. Looking back to Concord from the distances of past and future, Thoreau felt that *Walden* was not so much his quarrel with society, but an expiation. "Through our recovered innocence," he confessed, "we discern the innocence of our neighbors." He was willing to share his regeneration, for above the constant interplay of Walden and village, there hovered a vision of an ideal village that transcended both. In the radical sense of the word, Thoreau, who had given up the wilder pursuit of hunting for farming, was a civilizer.

When he came to build his hut—the container of his vital heat —Thoreau used second-hand materials and borrowed tools and showed his dependence on civilization. He did not abandon collective wisdom: his intention was to practice philosophy, to come directly at a conduct of life, that is, to simplify, or experience the solid satisfaction of knowing immediately the materials that made his life. He scrupulously accounts for these materials, he tells their history—where he got the boards, who used them and under what conditions. And James Collins' life in the shanty is implicitly contrasted with Thoreau's, especially in Thoreau's remark that he purified the boards by bleaching and warping them in the sun. He also acknowledged his debt for tools. He did not push his economy too far, to the verge of self-sufficiency that some believe necessary to a defense of *Walden* as social gospel. He said—and this is the only way of repaying one's social indebtedness—that he sharpened the tools by use. In a similar way, he applied the funded wisdom of man to his experiment on life. Individualist that he was, he often confirmed his experience by the experience of others: he made his use of the classics and scriptures, Indian lore and colonial history, pay their way. He was starting from scratch, but he knew that the materials were old.

The building of the hut is so thoroughly described because on the symbolic level it is the description of the building of the body for his soul. A generation that was read in Swedenborg might have been expected to see this correspondence. "It would be worth the while," Thoreau suggested, "to build still more deliberately than I did, considering, for instance, what foundation a door, a window, a cellar, a garret, have in the nature of man, and perchance never raising any superstructure until we found a better reason for it than our temporal necessities even." He was speaking the language of functionalism that Swedenborgianism had popularized; and after listing his previous shelters, he remarked that "this frame, so slightly clad, was a sort of crystallization around me, and reacted on the builder."

Thoreau built his hut as he needed it, to meet the progressing seasons of developing consciousness, a development which was as organic as the seasons. He subscribed to Emerson's use of the cycle of day and night as the symbol of the ebb and flow of inspiration and extended it to the seasons: "The day is an epitome of the year. The night is the winter, the morning and evenings are spring and fall, and the noon is the summer." In this way he also followed Emerson's "history" of consciousness. "The Greek," Emerson wrote, "was the age of observation; the Middle Age, that of fact and thought; ours, that of reflection and ideas." In *Walden*, Thoreau's development began in the summer, the season of the senses and of delicious out-of-door life. This was the period when he was in sympathetic communion with Nature, refreshed by the tonic of wildness. The chapters on "Sounds" and "Solitude" belong to this period, during which he enjoyed the atmospheric presence of Nature so essential to his inspiration. And the hut, which he began in the spring and first occupied at this time, was merely a frame through which Nature readily passed.

When the "north wind had already begun to cool the pond," Thoreau said that he first began to "inhabit my house." During the autumn season of harvest and preparation for winter, he lathed

and plastered; and finally as winter approached he built his fireplace and chimney, "the most vital part of the house. . . ." By the
fireside, in the period of reflection and inner life, he lingered most,
communing with his self.* It was the time of soul-searching, when
he cut through the pond's ice and saw that "its bright sanded
floor [was] the same as in the summer"; and before the ice broke
up he surveyed its bottom. Even in this desolate season Thoreau
looked for all the signs of spring's organic promise, and in the
representative anecdote of his despair, he told of Nature's sustaining power: "After a still winter night I awoke with the impression that some question had been put to me, which I had been
endeavoring in vain to answer in my sleep, as what—how—when—
where? But there was dawning Nature, in whom all creatures live,
looking in at my broad windows with serene and satisfied face,
and no questions on *her* lips. I awoke to an answered question, to
Nature and daylight." Even in the winter of his discontent, Nature
seemed to him to say " 'Forward' " and he could calmly await the
inevitable golden age of spring.

V

Rebirth came with spring. In one of the best sustained analogies
in transcendental writing, the chapter "Spring," Thoreau reported
ecstatically the translation of the frozen sand and clay of the railroad cut into the thawing streams of life. Looking at the sand
foliage—the work of an hour—he said that "I am affected as if . . .
I stood in the laboratory of the Artist who made the world and
me. . . ." The Artist of the world, like Thoreau and like Goethe
whom he had in mind, labored "with the idea inwardly" and its
correspondence, its flowering, was the leaf. Everywhere Thoreau
perceived this symbol of creation, and in ascending forms from the
sand, the animal body, the feathers and wings of birds, to the
"airy" butterfly. "Thus it seemed," he wrote, "that this one hill-
side illustrated the principle of all the operations of Nature. The
Maker of this earth but patented a leaf." And the moral Thoreau
drew from this illustration was the central law of his life, for it
was the law of renewal: "This earth is not a mere fragment of dead
history, stratum upon stratum like the leaves of a book, to be
studied by geologists and antiquarians chiefly, but living poetry
like the leaves of a tree, which precede flowers and fruit,—not a

---

* Hawthorne in "Peter Goldthwaite's Treasure" and Melville in "I and My
Chimney" also made imaginative use of the house and the chimney.

fossil earth, but a living earth; compared with whose great central life all animal and vegetable life is merely parasitic. Its throes will heave our exuviae from their graves." And furthermore the law applied to man and the higher society: "... the institutions upon it [the earth] are plastic like clay in the hands of the potter."

For Thoreau, who had found that the law of his life was the law of Life, these perceptions were the stuff of ecstasy. Reveling in the sound of the first sparrow, Thoreau wrote, "What at such a time are histories, chronologies, traditions, and all written revelations?" The spring had brought forth "the symbol of perpetual youth," the grass-blade; human life, having died down to its root, now put forth "its green blade to eternity." Walden Pond had begun to melt —"Walden was dead and is alive again." The change in the flowing sand, from excremental to spiritual, had also been accomplished in him by the discipline of purity: "The change from storm and winter to serene and mild weather, from dark and sluggish hours to bright and elastic ones." Like the dawning of inspiration this "memorable crisis" was "seemingly instantaneous at last." "Suddenly," Thoreau recorded that change, "an influx of light filled my house, though evening was at hand, and the clouds of winter still overhung it, and the eaves were dripping with sleety rain. I looked out of the window, and lo! where yesterday was cold grey ice there lay the transparent pond already calm and full of hope as in a summer evening, reflecting a summer evening sky in its bosom, though none was visible overhead, as if it had intelligence with some remote horizon. I heard a robin in the distance, the first I had heard for many a thousand years, methought, whose note I shall not forget for many a thousand more,—the same sweet and powerful song as of yore. . . . So I came in, and shut the door, and passed my first spring night in the woods."

With the coming of spring had come "the creation of Cosmos out of Chaos and the realization of the Golden Age." And with his renewal had come the vindication of his life of purity. He had recorded what he felt was nowhere recorded, "a simple and irrepressible satisfaction with the gift of life. . . ." He had suggested what the eye of the partridge symbolized to him, not merely "the purity of infancy, but a wisdom clarified by experience." He had recounted the experience of his purification so well that even the reader who accepts only the residual statement feels purified. "I do not say," he wisely wrote at the end of *Walden*, "that John or Jonathan will realize all this [the perfect summer life]; but such is the character of that morrow which mere lapse of time can never make to dawn." To affirm this eternal present, to restore, as he said in "The Service," the original of which Nature is the reflection, he fashioned *Walden* as he himself lived, after the example of the artist of the city of Kouroo. This parable unlocks the largest meaning of the book. The artist of Kouroo "was disposed to strive after perfection," Thoreau wrote; and striving, he lived in the eternity of inspiration which made the passing of dynasties, even eras, an illusion. In fashioning his staff, merely by minding his destiny and his art, he had made a new world "with full and fair proportions." The result, Thoreau knew, could not be "other than wonderful," because "the material was pure, and his art was pure. . . ."

R. W. B. Lewis

The Case against the Past

"We have the Saint Vitus dance." This was Thoreau's view of the diversion of energies to material expansion and of the enthusiastic arithmetic by which expansion was constantly being measured. Miles of post roads and millions of tons of domestic export did not convince Thoreau that first principles ought to be overhauled; but a close interest in these matters did convince him that first principles had been abandoned. Probably nobody of his generation had a richer sense of the potentiality for a fresh, free, and uncluttered existence; certainly no one projected the need for the ritual burning of the past in more varied and captivating metaphors. This is what *Walden* is about; it is the most searching contemporary account of the desire for a new kind of life. But Thoreau's announcement of a spiritual molting season (one of his favorite images) did not arise from a belief that the building of railroads was proof of the irrelevance of too-well-remembered doctrines. Long before Whitman, himself a devotee of the dazzling sum, attacked the extremes of commercialism in *Democratic Vistas,*

Reprinted from *The American Adam* (Chicago: The University of Chicago Press, 1955), pp. 20–27, by permission of the author and the publisher. Copyright 1955 by The University of Chicago Press.

Thoreau was insisting that the obsession with railroads did not demonstrate the hope for humanity, but tended to smother it. "Men think it is essential that the *Nation* have commerce, and export ice, and talk through a telegraph and ride thirty miles an hour, without a doubt, whether *they* do or not; but whether we should live like baboons or men is a little uncertain."

Watching the local railroad train as it passed near Walden Pond on the recently laid track between Fitchburg and Boston, Thoreau noticed that while the narrow little cars moved eastward along the ground, the engine smoke drifted skyward, broadening out as it rose. The picture (it occurs in the chapter called "Sounds") provided him with a meaningful glimpse of that wholeness, of interrelated doubleness, which was for Thoreau the required shape of the life that was genuinely lived. The trouble with railroads—he said it, in fancy, to the scores of workmen he saw starting up in protest against him—was that so few persons who rode on them were heading in any definite direction or were aware of a better direction than Boston; quite a few persons were simply run over, while the building of railroads crushed the heart and life out of the builders. The trouble, in general, with expending one's strength on "internal improvements" was that the achievement, like the aim, was partial: there was nothing internal about them. The opportunity that Thoreau looked out upon from his hut at Walden was for no such superficial accomplishment, but for a wholeness of spirit realized in a direct experience of the whole of nature. The words "nature" and "wholeness" have been overworked and devitalized (Thoreau and Emerson are partly to blame), and now they are suspect; but they glow with health in the imaginatively ordered prose of Henry Thoreau.

The narrator of *Walden* is a witness to a truly new world which the speaker alone has visited, from which he has just returned, and which he is sure every individual ought to visit at least once—not the visible world around Walden Pond, but an inner world which the Walden experience allowed him to explore. Thoreau liked to pretend that his book was a purely personal act of private communion. But that was part of his rhetoric, and *Walden* is a profoundly rhetorical book, emerging unmistakably from the long New England preaching tradition; though here the trumpet call announces the best imaginable news rather than apocalyptic warnings. Thoreau, in *Walden*, is a man who has come back down into the cave to tell the residents there that they are really in chains, suffering fantastic punishments they have imposed on themselves, seeing by a light that is reflected and derivative. A major test of the visionary hero must always be the way he can put his experience to work for the benefit of mankind; he demonstrates his freedom in the liberation of others. Thoreau prescribes the following cure: the total renunciation of the traditional, the conventional, the socially acceptable, the well-worn paths of conduct, and the total immersion in nature.

Everything associated with the past should be burned away. The past should be cast off like dead skin. Thoreau remembered with sympathetic humor the pitiful efforts of one John Field, an Irishman living at near-by Baker Farm, to catch perch with shiners: "thinking to live by some derivative old-country mode in this primitive new country." "I look on England today," he wrote, "as an old gentleman who is travelling with a great deal of baggage, trumpery which has accumulated from long housekeeping, which he has not the courage to burn." Thoreau recorded with approval and some envy a Mexican purification rite practiced every fifty-two years; and he added, "I have scarcely heard of a truer sacrament." These periodic symbolic acts of refreshment, which whole societies ought to perform in each generation ("One generation abandons the enterprises of another like stranded vessels"), were valid exactly because they were images of fundamental reality itself. Individuals and groups should enact the rhythmic death and rebirth reflected in the change of season from winter to spring, in the sequence of night and day. "The phenomena of the year take place every day in a pond on a small scale." These were some of the essential facts discovered by Thoreau when he fronted them at Walden; and the experience to which he was to become a witness took its shape, in act and in description, from a desire to live in accordance with these facts. So it was that he refused the offer of a door-mat, lest he should form the habit of shaking it every morning; and, instead, every morning "I got up early and bathed in the pond; that was a religious exercise, and one of the best things which I did."

The language tells us everything, as Thoreau meant it to. He had his own sacramental system, his own rite of baptism. But his use of the word "nature" indicates that the function of sacraments was to expose the individual again to the currents flowing through nature, rather than to the grace flowing down from supernature. The ritual of purification was no less for Thoreau than for St. Paul a dying into life; but Thoreau marched to the music he heard; it was the music of the age; and he marched in a direction *opposite* to St. Paul. His familiar witticism, "One world at a time" (made on his deathbed to an eager abolitionist named Pillsbury, who looked for some illumination of the future life from the dying seer) was a fair summary of his position: with this addition, that poetry traditionally taken as hints about what could be seen through a glass darkly about the next world was taken by Thoreau as what had been seen by genius, face to face with this one. He was among the first to see Christian literature as only the purest and most inspiring of the fables about the relation of man to nature and about the infinite capacities of the unaided human spirit. The Bible (Thoreau referred to it simply as "an old book") was the finest poem which had ever been written; it was the same in substance as Homeric or Hindu mythology, but it was richer in metaphor. The Bible spoke more sharply to the human condition. This was why Thoreau, like Whitman, could employ the most traditional of religious phrases and invest them with an unexpected and dynamic new life.

It is not surprising that transcendentalism was Puritanism turned upside down, as a number of critics have pointed out; historically, it could hardly have been anything else. Transcendentalism drew on the vocabularies of European romanticism and Oriental mysticism; but the only available local vocabulary was the one that the hopeful were so anxious to escape from, and a very effective way to discredit its inherited meaning was to serve it up in an unfamiliar context. There was something gratifyingly shocking in such a use of words: "What demon possessed me that I behaved so well?" Thoreau spoke as frequently as he could, therefore, about a *sacrament*, a sacred mystery, such as baptism: in order to define the cleansing, not of St. Paul's natural man, but of the conventional or traditional man; in order, precisely, to bring into being the natural man. For the new tensions out of which insights were drawn and moral choices provoked were no longer the relation of nature and grace, of man and God, but of the natural and the artificial, the new and the old, the individual and the social or conventional. Thoreau had, as he remarked in his other deathbed witticism, no quarrel with God; his concern was simply other.

His concern was with the strangulation of nature by convention. The trouble with conventions and traditions in the New World was that they had come first; they had come from abroad and from a very long way back; and they had been superimposed upon nature. They had to be washed away, like sin, so that the natural could reveal itself again and could be permitted to create its own organic conventions. They had to be renounced, as the first phase of the ritual; and if renunciation was, as Emily Dickinson thought, a piercing virtue, it was not because it made possible an experience of God in an infusion of grace, but because it made possible an experience of self in a bath of nature.

Thoreau had, of course, learned a good deal from Emerson, whose early energy was largely directed toward constructing "an original relation with the universe" and who reverted time and again to the same theme: "beware of tradition"; "forget historical Christianity"; "lop off all superfluity and tradition, and fall back on the nature of things." And what was this nature of things which men were enjoined to fall back on? Lowell understood some of it, in one of the better sentences of his querulous and uneven essay on Thoreau (1865): "There is only one thing better than tradition, and that is the original and eternal life out of which all tradition takes its rise. It was this life which the reformers demanded, with more or less clearness of consciousness and expression, life in politics, life in literature, life in religion." But even in this moment of qualified approval, Lowell makes it sound too pallid, soft, and ethereal. Nature was not merely the mountains and the prairie, any more than it was merely the bees and the flowers; but it was all of those things too, and it must always include them. If nature was partly represented by "Higher Laws," as the title of one chapter in *Walden* tells us, it was represented also by "Brute Neighbors," "Winter Animals," and a "Bean-Field," as we know from the titles of other chapters. Thoreau's nature is bounded by an irony which applies the phrase "Higher Laws" to a chapter that, for all its idealism, talks at some length about fried rats.

Irony too—the doubleness of things—Thoreau could learn from Emerson, as each of them had learned from Coleridge and Plato. "All the universe over," Emerson wrote in his journal (1842), "there is just one thing, this old double." The old double, the ideal and the actual, the higher law and the fried rat, required a double consciousness and found expression in a double criticism; nature could be satisfied with nothing else. Emerson tramped in mud puddles, and Thoreau, more adventurously, swam in Walden Pond; the puddle and the pond were instances of unimpeded nature; but both men searched, in their separate ways, for the spiritual analogues which completed the doubleness of nature. Their ability to address themselves with very nearly equal fluency to both dimensions of consciousness gave later comfort to idealists and nominalists alike, though neither group understood the Emersonian principle that only the whole truth could be true at all. Bronson Alcott was the most high-minded of the contemporary idealists, but Emerson chided him for neglecting the value of the many in his rapture for the one, and thought he had genius but no talent. "The philosophers of Fruitlands," Emerson said in 1843, naming Alcott's experimental community, "have such an image of virtue before their eyes, that the poetry of man and nature they never see; the poetry that is man's life, the poorest pastoral clownish life; the light that shines on a man's hat, in a child's spoon." He was harder, of course, on those who saw only the hat and the spoon: the materialists and the tradesmen whom he excoriated in many essays, and writers who stuck too obstinately to the ordinary (Emerson would say, the "vulgar") aspects of the visible world.

Thoreau's personal purification rite began with the renunciation of old hats and old spoons and went forward to the moment—as he describes himself in the opening paragraph of "Higher Laws"— when the initiate stood fully alive in the midst of nature, eating a woodchuck with his fingers, and supremely aware, at the same instant, of the higher law of virtue. "I love the wild not less than the good," Thoreau admitted, announcing duplicity in his own peculiar accent. The structure of *Walden* has a similar beginning and a similar motion forward. The book starts amid the punishing conventions of Concord, departs from them to the pond and the forest, explores the natural surroundings, and exposes the natural myth of the yearly cycle, to conclude with the arrival of spring, the full possession of life, and a representative anecdote about the sudden bursting into life of a winged insect long buried in an old table of apple-tree wood.[1]

Individual chapters are sometimes carried along to the same rhythm. "Sounds," for example, starts with conventional signs and then looks to nature for more authentic ones; it picks up the cycle of the day, as Thoreau listens to sounds around the clock; and it concludes with a total surrender to the vitalizing power of unbounded nature. Thoreau had been talking about his reading in the previous chapter; now he reminds us: "While we are confined to books . . . we are in danger of forgetting the language which all things and events speak without metaphor." Sounds are elements of this natural language: the sound of the trains passing in the

---

[1] I am indebted here to the analysis of *Walden* as a rebirth ritual by Stanley Hyman, "Henry Thoreau in Our Time," *Atlantic Monthly,* CLXXVIII (November, 1946), 137–46. Mr. Hyman acknowledges his own debt, which I share, to F. O. Matthiessen's treatment of Thoreau in *American Renaissance* (New York, 1941).

morning; the church bells from Lincoln, Bedford, or Concord; the lowing of cows in the evening; "regularly at half-past seven," the vesper chant of the whip-poor-wills; the "maniacal hooting of owls," which "represent the stark twilight and unsatisfied thoughts which all have"; "late in the evening . . . the distant rumbling of wagons over bridges,—a sound heard farther than almost any other at night,—the baying of dogs . . . the trump of bullfrogs"; and then at dawn the morning song of the cockerel, the lusty call to awaken of the chanticleer which Thoreau offered on the title-page as the symbol of the book. "To walk in a winter morning, in a wood where these birds abounded . . . think of it! It would put nations on the alert." Finally, in a morning mood, Thoreau closes his chapter rejoicing that his hut has no yard, no fence, but is part of unfenced nature itself.

It was with the ultimate aim of making such an experience possible—a life determined by nature and enriched by a total awareness—that Thoreau insisted so eloquently upon the baptismal or rebirth rite. What he was demanding was that individuals start life all over again, and that in the new world a fresh start was literally and immediately possible to anyone wide enough awake to attempt it. It was in this way that the experience could also appear as a return to childhood, to the scenes and the wonder of that time. In a particularly revealing moment, Thoreau reflected, while adrift on the lake in the moonlight and playing the flute for the fishes, on a boyhood adventure at that very place. "But now," he said, "I made my home by the shore." Thoreau reflected the curious but logical reverence of his age for children: "Children, who play life, discern its true law and relations more clearly than men, who fail to live it worthily." Children seemed for Thoreau to possess some secret which had been lost in the deadening process of growing up, some intimation (like Wordsworth's child) which had faded under the routine pressure of everyday life. Emerson found the new attitude of adults toward children the appropriate symbol with which to introduce his retrospective summary of the times (1867): "Children had been repressed and kept in the background; now they were considered, cosseted and pampered." Thoreau thought he knew why: because "every child begins the world again"; every child managed to achieve without conscious effort what the adult could achieve only by the strenuous, periodic act of refreshment. In this sense, the renewal of life was a kind of homecoming; the busks and the burnings were preparatory to recapturing the outlook of children.

Psychologists who have followed Jung's poetic elaboration and doctrinaire schematizing of the guarded suggestions of Freud could make a good deal of the impulse. They might describe it as an impulse to return to the womb; and some support could doubtless be found in the image-clusters of Walden: water, caves, shipwrecks, and the like. This approach might persuasively maintain that the end of the experience narrated by Thoreau was the reintegration of the personality. And since, according to Jung, "the lake in the valley is the unconscious," it is possible to hold that *Walden* enacts and urges the escape from the convention-ridden conscious and the release of the spontaneous energies of personality lying beneath the surface, toward a reuniting of the psychic "old double." An analysis of this sort can be helpful and even illuminating, and it could be applied to the entire program of the party of Hope, substituting terms associated with the unconscious for all the terms associated with Emerson's "Reason." A certain warrant for the psychological interpretation can be found in the novels of Dr. Holmes, and the methodological issue arises more sharply in that discussion. But we may also remind ourselves that the psychological vocabulary simply manipulates a set of metaphors other than those we normally use. Probably we do not need to go so far afield to grasp what Thoreau was seeking to explain; we may even suspect that he meant what he said. And what he said was that he went to the woods in order to live deliberately, "to front only the essential facts of life"; because human life and human expression were so burdened with unexamined habits, the voice of experience so muffled by an uninvestigated inheritance, that only by a total rejection of those habits and that inheritance and by a recovery of a childlike wonder and directness could anyone find out whether life were worth living at all.

Thoreau, like most other members of the hopeful party, understood dawn and birth better than he did night and death. He responded at once to the cockerel in the morning; the screech owls at night made him bookish and sentimental. And though their wailing spoke to him about "the low spirits and melancholy forebodings of fallen souls," the whole dark side of the world was no more than another guaranty of the inexhaustible variety of nature.[2] Thoreau knew not evil; his American busk would have fallen short, like the

---

[2] Thoreau goes on to say that the hooting of owls "is a sound admirably suited to swamps and twilight woods which no day illustrates, suggesting a vast and undeveloped nature which men have not yet recognized." The figurative language here is suggestive and may be surprising to anyone who supposes Thoreau unaware of the very existence of the cloacal regions of mind and nature.

bonfire in Hawthorne's fantasy, of the profounder need for the purification of the human heart. He would have burned away the past as the accumulation of artifice, in the name of the natural and the essential. But if the natural looked to him so much more wholesome and so much more dependable than others have since thought it, his account of the recovery of nature was never less than noble: the noblest expression, in fact and in language, of the first great aspiration of the age.

Perry Miller

Thoreau in the Context of International Romanticism

... To read the "Preface" with Thoreau in mind is to realize anew how different was the situation of the Romantic revolutionary in England (as indeed in all Europe) from that of the American. The chief thrust of Wordsworth is against the poetic diction of the Neo-Classical age, the formalized and stereotyped abstract adjectives of Pope and Johnson. His great plea is that poetry use "the real language of men." We comprehend from his fervent argument how terribly dominating Neo-Classical verse had been in literary England. Provincial America endeavored to imitate the mode—witness Freneau and the Connecticut Wits—but we never had a poet who so tyrannized over our native taste as did Pope in England. Hence when youths like Emerson felt the impulse from the vernal wood stirring in their hearts, they had to exert themselves not so much in dethroning a vested interest in technique as merely in liberating themselves from a culture that they now perceived was prosaic and uncreative. They simply had to disassociate themselves from what Emerson pungently called "the corpse-cold Unitarianism of Brattle Street and Harvard College."

Reprinted by permission of the publishers from Perry Miller, *Nature's Nation* (Cambridge, Mass.: The Belknap Press of Harvard University Press, 1967), pp. 179–83. Copyright, 1967, by the President and Fellows of Harvard College. Previously published in *The New England Quarterly*, XXXIV (June 1961), 147–59.

Or, like Henry, they could resign from all the societies they had never joined—including the Thoreau Society!

Hence what meant the most to them in Wordsworth's "Preface" were the hints he threw out about a new kind of utterance—he was talking about poetry but his prescriptions would apply as well to prose—in which the writer would strive by might and main to look steadily at his subject. The most thrilling paragraph to the generation of Thoreau would be that wherein Wordsworth rejected as idle and unmanly the faintness of heart which, despairing of ever producing a language as fitting for expression of the passion as the real passion itself, abjectly concluded that the artist should become a translator and substitute excellencies of another kind for those which are unattainable in speech. By this specious attempt to surpass his subject, said Wordsworth, the writer condemns his material to an inferior status, and thus slyly exalts himself over it. No, no: fidelity to the thing, strict application to the object, no underestimation of the value of the fact—these convictions and only these will create a literature "not standing upon external testimony, but carried alive into the heart by passion; truth which is its own testimony, which gives competence and confidence to the tribunal to which it appeals, and receives them from the same tribunal."

As we know, Wordsworth had a long struggle explaining to his contemporaries that by his phrases "the language really spoken by men" and his "looking steadily at the subject" he did not mean what we would term photographic reproduction of the scene or of the human face. Romantic Nature was not—for better or for worse —what the next generation would salute as "Realism." Wordsworth never taught the neophyte that a daguerreotype of Walden Pond should be esteemed more highly than a truly poetic rendition of it. He insisted that poetry have form, that it cast into metrical arrangements the materials carried alive into the heart, that passion come into literature not as animal cries or exclamations of pain, but as emotion recollected in tranquility. This meant that while no *a priori* concept of the picturesque, or of dignity or of excellence, should be imposed from without, that there would be an organic growth of the concept out of a fervent devotion to objective truth. The fact, in other words, would flower into a truth— *if*, that is, the poet could bring an adequate passion to his portraitture. Thoreau, therefore, would not be betraying or patronizing or insulting his material when he openly admitted that he was "for convenience putting the experience of two years into one." That was not illegitimate manipulation of reality, it was a way of being "something more than natural," of becoming "Nature's brother."

By the time Thoreau graduated from Harvard, this Romantic aesthetic had been widely domesticated in America. The principal agent in reconciling a suspicious public to what had at first seemed a nonsensical or even subversive paradox was landscape painting. In terms comprehensible to the average intelligence the Hudson River School, as historians now label them, were dramatizing Wordsworth's great "Idea." Indeed, I am convinced that one immensely helpful way to deepen our appreciation of what Thoreau was seeking is to look closely at certain pictures of Thomas Cole (not his grandiose tableaus but his smaller scenes), Asher Durand or Thomas Doughty. Especially I would say Durand, for in him appears that union of graphic detail and organizing design which the disciple of Wordsworth ever strove to attain. An influential periodical of the time, the *Knickerbocker*, said of him in 1853— just as *Walden* was receiving its last revision—that "His compositions, while faithful to the truth of detail, combine a beautiful *sentiment*, which is felt by the observer, and it is in this in which his true greatness consists." All the implications of this sentence, advertised by its use of "while" along with "combine," show how, even in the complacent circles which subscribed to the *Knickerbocker*, the Romantic "Idea" had become an orthodoxy. Hence the more opulent in these circles paid high prices for the landscapes of Durand and his fellows. We might surmise that by the same token they should have recognized in *Walden* a prose counterpart to their beloved painters. But, as is a matter of record, they bought the paintings but never the book.

There are a hundred reasons why comfortable citizens of the Republic in 1854 would hang over their fireplace a landscape by Durand or Doughty, at the wildness of which they might gaze without perturbation, and still be horrified at the wildness of *Walden*—if indeed they so much as heard of it. Among these reasons, however, must be enumerated—or at least I shall venture to list it—the fact that Thoreau managed so radical a penetration into "the truth of detail," and then so blatant an assertion of what the *Knickerbocker* called "sentiment," that the "combination"— to use again the catchword of the era—seemed either grotesque or truly demoniacal. Or another way to put it is to say that Henry Thoreau took the basic premise of the Romantic Age more seriously than most romantics were able to accept.

I would not unduly belabor this point, yet I would like to suggest that it indicates the perennial and never quite definable fascination of *Walden*. Thoreau spoke it as bluntly as possible in the chapter he called "Sounds," and most succinctly in the first sentence. Books, he there said, are things in dialect and are provincial, and if we are confined solely to them, "we are in danger of forgetting the language which all things and events speak without metaphor, which alone is copious and standard." Consequently *Walden* is one of the supreme achievements of the Romantic Movement—or to speak accurately, of Romantic Naturalism. Mr. Shanley has proved beyond the shadow of any doubt that it was a conscious, a deliberate creation; it was not and is not some spontaneous impulse from the vernal wood, although unfortunately many of its modern champions pretend that it was. No, it is truly emotion, but emotion ostensibly recollected in tranquility. Yet it is assuredly emotion, passion. There is no substitution for the original experience, there are no excellencies of diction contrived so as to suggest an inferiority of the original to the narration. Still, it is not a mere recital, item by item, atomic moment after moment, of two years beside the pond. It is a magnificent autobiography, faithful in every detail to the setting, arising to the level of a treatise on imagination and taste, and all this without ever becoming didactic. When seen in such a perspective, it can be placed beside *The Prelude*. It is the "growth of a poet's mind," and despite all its wealth of concrete imagery it is centered not upon Nature, but upon Nature's brother, the intelligence of the artist.

I need hardly observe that in this century the entire philosophy of what I call Romantic Naturalism has been attacked from innumerable sides and is generally thought to be completely discredited. In painting, the Hudson River School of representation gave way to a succession of infinitely more sophisticated methods until eventually the object disappeared altogether and an artist simply painted his idea. In poetry the creative impulse for several decades has been calling for a repudiation of the identification of mind with thing, for the formulation of a poetry which shall be entirely intellectual, metaphorical, artificial. That disposition which in recent English writing has been expressed in Yeats, in Ezra Pound, in T. S. Eliot, sees in the artist a manipulator, an inventor of symbols and images, who severs himself from Nature, who deliberately violates her, pillages her for schemes of his own devising. And even Robert Frost, who like Wordsworth insists that poetry must keep close to the language of ordinary human talk, reminds us again and again that we must avoid the pathetic fallacy of assuming any correspondence between human emotions and natural fact. If one is versed in country things, he memorably says, one does not suppose phoebes weep over the desolation of an abandoned farmhouse. Indeed, in one of his most powerful proclamations, "The Most of It," Frost seems to be deriding all the Henry Thoreaus of his past by describing a "he" who kept the universe alone, who wanted from Nature "someone else additional to him" and who received in answer only the sudden eruption from the woods of a great buck, an utterly inhuman beast.

If the twentieth-century judgment of the Romantic aesthetic is correct, then Henry Thoreau is one of its monumental failures and martyrs, along with Shelley and Novalis. Neither he nor they were able to answer the terrible question of whether, once they committed themselves to the proposition that their most delicate experience was typified in Nature, they were thereafter actually writing about Nature—about Walden Pond, for instance—or about nothing more than their delicious experiences. If in reality they were only projecting their emotions onto the Natural setting, if the phoebes do not weep for human miseries, then their effort to find someone additional to themselves was doomed to ghastly defeat. In this view, the career of Henry Thoreau is as tragic as that of King Lear. He too sacrificed himself needlessly to a delusion.

In his first organized statement, Thoreau could say, with all the confidence that a Lear had in the love of his daughters, that when he detects a beauty in any recess of Nature he is reminded of the inexpressible privacy of a life, that he may rest content with nothing more than the sight and the sound. On the premise of that doctrine, he may properly say no more than "I am affected by the sight of the cabins of muskrats," or than "I am the wiser in respect to all knowledges, and better qualified for all fortunes, for knowing that there is a minnow in the brook." In the glowing confidence of these aphorisms lurks the assumption that moral law and natural law contain analogies, and that for this reason the writer may safely record facts without metaphors, since truths are bound to sprout from them. The later portions of Thoreau's *Journal*, those after 1854, with their tedious recordings of mere observations, of measurements, of statistics, seem to attest not only the dwindling of his vitality but the exhaustion of the theory upon which he commenced to be an author in the first place. He immolated himself on the pyre of an untenable concept of literary creation.

And yet, he refuses to be consumed. Expound *Walden*, if you will, as a temporary and so an empty triumph of the Romantic dream, as a work doomed to diminish with the recession of that dream, yet the book refuses to go into the archeological oblivion of, shall I say? Shelley's *The Revolt of Islam.* Robert Frost, while objecting with all his Yankee soul to Thoreau's epistemology, still proclaims that with him Thoreau is a "passion." The obvious answer, or rather the easy one, is that Thoreau was a great writer, and so his pages survive in spite of changes in metophysical fashions. But that is truly an easy, a luxurious way of salvaging our poet. The more difficult, but I believe the more honest and, in the final accounting, the more laudatory way is to say that the Romantic balance, or its "Idea" of combination, of fusing the fact and the idea, the specific and the general, is still a challenge to the mind and to the artist. Thoreau was *both* a Transcendentalist and a Natural Historian. He never surrendered on either front, though the last years of the *Journal* show how desperate was the effort to keep both standards aloft. He said, in the central conceptual passage of *Walden*, that he wanted to drive life into a corner, to publish its meanness if it proved to be mean, but that if it should turn out to be sublime, then to give a true account of its sublimity. "The universe constantly and obediently answers to our conceptions" was his resolute determination. For what more sublime a cause, even though it be a questionable thesis, can a man expend himself?

John C. Broderick

The Movement of Thoreau's Prose

... Thoreau's writings, like *Leaves of Grass,* are full of movement, are on the go. The "walk" supplies structural thread for "Walking," "A Walk to Wachusett," "A Winter Walk," and *Cape Cod.* The extended walk or "journey" serves for *The Maine Woods,*

Reprinted from *American Literature,* XXXIII (May 1961), 133–42, by permission of the author and Duke University Press.

A Week on the Concord and Merrimack Rivers, a "water walk" with occasional scrambling along the bank. Even "Civil Disobedience" records what its author calls "a long journey," the result of "traveling into a far country," and the dislocations of life arraigned in "Slavery in Massachusetts" symbolically culminate in this: "The remembrance of my country spoils my walk." (The surprisingly optimistic conclusion of the latter essay is occasioned by a white water-lily, "the emblem of purity," discovered on a walk.) *Walden* itself might be regarded as a year-long walk, for as in his daily walk Thoreau moved away from the mundane world of the village toward one of heightened awareness and potentiality, only to return spiritually reinvigorated, so *Walden* records an adventuring on life which structurally starts from and returns to the world of quiet desperation.

Thoreau has rarely received credit for such compositional excellence in large matters. James Russell Lowell spoke of his inability to sustain a work "to the serene balance of completeness" while praising his "exquisite mechanical skill" in the sentence or the paragraph.[1] The distinction has remained viable, despite considerable recent interest in Thoreau's structures. His writing is still likely to be described by friendly critics as a "mosaic" or "montage." One of the best, while comparing the writing to "an Indian's quiet tread, covering ground, making distance," nonetheless considers Thoreau "essentially an aphorist whose unit of writing was the epigrammatic sentence."[2] Thoreau's best paragraphs, however, do not depend entirely on "the personality of the writer" for their unity. Instead, they move as Thoreau did and as his books do—from the mundane known to the transcendent knowable and back again. By various stylistic means he involves the reader in an intense spirtual experience, only to set him down again in the world from which he has been removed, presumably with more abundant resources for living.

A fairly simple example of such writing is the first paragraph of *Walden:*

> When I wrote the following pages, or rather the bulk of them, I lived alone, in the woods, a mile from any neighbor, in a house which I had built myself, on the shore of Walden Pond, in Concord, Massachusetts, and earned my living by the labor of my

---

[1] James Russell Lowell, *Writings,* Riverside Ed. (Boston and New York, 1892), I, 370.
[2] Reginald L. Cook, *Passage to Walden* (Boston, 1949), pp. 220–225.

hands only. I lived there two years and two months. At present
I am a sojourner in civilized life again.[3]

The paragraph begins deceptively, especially since the disarming
qualification, "or rather the bulk of them," suggests a characteristic
fastidiousness about fact which authenticates *Walden* as a whole.
But the remainder of the first sentence comprises a series of short
phrasal units, all but one of which ("in Concord, Massachusetts")
puts the "I" at greater and greater remoteness from the world of
the ordinary reader, removed by solitude, by locality, by personal
construction of his dwelling, and by activity—manual labor. The
last two sentences of the paragraph mark the return. The second
sentence suggests that the distancing experience had temporal
limits (a suggestion implicit in the first three words of the paragraph; we have also been reassured by "Concord, Massachusetts").
The last sentence "places" the "I," but there is ambiguity in the
word "sojourner," suggesting that his return may be only temporary, that like Melville's Bulkington he may soon ship on another
voyage, that he has not passively renewed ordinary obligations.
The paragraph, in short, is a miniature of *Walden* as a whole.

In its "out-and-back" movement the paragraph is typical, but
in its simplicity of means it is less so. Many of Thoreau's paragraphs have the same movement but employ more complicated devices. Such paragraphs often begin with deceptively simple, largely
monosyllabic utterances which are succeeded by poetic, allusive,
metaphorical enrichment before the return. But the closing sentence—often humorous—serves two functions: it completes the
release, but it also recalls the journey just completed. Meanwhile,
during the journey Thoreau has kept his reader aware of starting
point and destination. Puns, irony, quirky quotations and allusions, careful etymologies—these are a few of his devices to relieve
some of the tension of the journey and forecast release from its
spiritual intensity.

The most concentrated example of such writing may be an
amusing, rather trivial paragraph near the end of "Economy" in
Walden:

Not long since I was present at the auction of a deacon's effects,
for his life had not been ineffectual:—

"The evil that men do lives after them."

As usual, a great proportion was trumpery which had begun to

---

[3] Henry David Thoreau, *Writings,* Walden Ed. (Boston and New York,
1906), II, 3.

accumulate in his father's day. Among the rest was a dried tape-worm. And now, after lying half a century in his garret and other dust holes, these things were not burned; instead of a *bonfire,* or purifying destruction of them, there was an *auction,* or increasing of them. The neighbors eagerly collected to view them, bought them all, and carefully transported them to their garrets and dust holes, to lie there till their estates are settled, when they will start again. When a man dies he kicks the dust.[4]

The spiritual exhortation of the paragraph is slight, emerging chiefly from the negative examples of "desperation" concerning furnishings. But almost all the devices are here: the pun ("in-effectual"), the familiar quotation eccentrically used, the etymolog-ically exact play on *auction* and *bonfire.* The sheer ingenuity of these words and phrases prompts a double response, in which amusement softens the ardors of the better life and actually secures these ardors a hearing. But the most effective sentence is the last, in which the familiar folk remark cuts two ways. Its familiarity is reassuring (even the low-keyed demands of this paragraph are ultimately impracticable). But its metaphoric aptness ("dust" is a favorite term of Thoreau's for what is wrong with life) sets up reverberations which echo the demands for a life of sanity and principle, even at the moment of release from absolute insistence upon it.

One of the most justly famous passages in *Walden* is that sub-lime apologia for life in the woods.

I went to the woods because I wished to live deliberately, to front only the essential facts of life, and see if I could not learn what it had to teach, and not, when I came to die, discover that I had not lived. I did not wish to live what was not life, living is so dear; nor did I wish to practise resignation, unless it was quite necessary. I wanted to live deep and suck out all the marrow of life, to live so sturdily and Spartanlike as to put to rout all that was not life, to cut a broad swath and shave close, to drive life into a corner, and reduce it to its lowest terms, and, if it proved to be mean, why then to get the whole and genuine meanness of it, and publish its meanness to the world; or if it were sublime, to know it by experience, and be able to give a true account of it in my next excursion. For most men, it appears to me, are in a strange uncertainty about it, whether it is of the devil or of God, and have *somewhat hastily* concluded that it is the chief end of man here to "glorify God and enjoy him forever." [5]

---

[4] *Writings,* II, 75.
[5] *Writings,* II, 100–101.

An intense paragraph like this provides little comfort for the man unwilling to accept the most strenuous demands of the moral life; but there is some. The first sentence, like its author, begins deliberately, then mounts and mounts—to an ironic climax. The ultimate distinction of the idealist between "life" and "not life" is nonetheless presented in a verbally playful way. The slightly humorous qualifications of the next sentence ("living is so dear" and "unless it was quite necessary") provide additional momentary relief before we are confronted with that remarkable series of metaphors for life at its best. We have passed Conantum and Nine-Acre Corner now; we are at Walden itself. The language which records the author's fronting of life at "its lowest terms" (really the highest) has forced the reader to a similar fronting. The excitement, the challenge, the appeal are almost unbearable. But we cannot live at Walden forever. To perpetuate such godlike moments would require transfiguration of the human condition. Mercifully, the author initiates a return by the parallel qualifications, "if it proved to be . . . or if it were . . . ." The jocularity of "my next excursion" distances both author and reader from the epiphany only recently shared. The joke continues with the powerful extravagance of the next sentence (ironically balanced by the modest "it appears to me"), but the last words of the paragraph are "glorify God and enjoy him forever," words almost meaningless in their reassuring familiarity. The sojourner through this paragraph, however, has had a glimpse of the glory itself, and for him life (and the stale quotation) can never be exactly the same as before he entered the woods.

The long paragraph following this one in *Walden* reveals other stylistic means of departure and safe return: playful allusions to classical myth and fable (ants and men, pygmies and cranes) and the straight-faced drollery connected with the extended pun on "sleepers." Between these is the almost strident recommendation of "simplicity." In such a passage as that on simplicity, Thoreau loses some of the aesthetic detachment which he elsewhere maintains, but his functional stylistic devices enable the reader, at least, to enter and leave the paragraph with profit and without embarrassment. The companion passage in "Conclusion" in *Walden* ("I left the woods . . ." and the paragraph following) has roughly the same movement, out and back, culminating: "If you have built castles in the air, your work need not be lost; that is where they should be. Now put the foundations under them." Here we emerge almost with a blueprint for approximating in ordinary life the glimpsed reality in art of Romantic idealism.

And there are similar passages: such familiar paragraphs in *Walden* as those beginning "The mass of men lead lives of quiet desperation" ("Economy") and "With thinking we may be beside ourselves in a sane sense" ("Solitude"); that in *A Week* beginning "The New Testament is an invaluable book" ("Sunday"); the paragraph in "Walking" from which the epigraph is taken; and others. Thoreau's highly charged polemical writing ("Civil Disobedience," "Slavery in Massachusetts," and "A Plea for Captain John Brown"), on the other hand, has many paragraphs in which the author provides a journey without a return, working instead toward a more conventional climax. And, needless to say, a great many paragraphs do not reveal this kind of movement at all. But a surprising amount of Thoreau's best remembered and most effective writing through analysis displays its stylistic kinship to the well-loved walk.

Walden as a whole has recently surrendered its dynamic structural secret, in which the movement of the book is associated with the rhythm of the seasons. Still obscure, however, is the nature of some subordinate "movements," embracing several chapters. For example, after explaining where "I" lived and what "I" lived for, Thoreau treats first "Reading," an activity closely associated with civilized life, moves next to "Sounds," many of which still remind him of the village but which progressively and inexorably lead him (and us) further and further into the intense, distancing experience available in "Solitude," which culminates in the account of mystical visits from "the old settler and original proprietor," God himself. An almost too startling return from this high moment begins in the next chapter, "Visitors," the first paragraph of which incongruously, we almost feel *irreverently*, associates the saintly hero of *Walden* with a "bar-room." And the return is completed two chapters later in "The Village," a momentary return (the shortest chapter in *Walden*) before renewing the memorable journey.

At the very center of *Walden* is a troublesome but important chapter called "Higher Laws," which re-echoes some of the objectionable stridency of earlier passages. It nevertheless clearly contains a very intense spiritual exhortation in which fishing is associated with the primitive or wild and the renunciation of animal food with the spiritual or higher nature. The next chapter, "Brute Neighbors," commences with a comic, ironic dialogue between Poet and Hermit, in which the hermit must choose between going "to heaven or a-fishing." He eventually casts for the latter, sure that there "never is but one opportunity of a kind." Astute readers have recognized here some kind of descent, but this particular descent is merely one more example of the Thoreauvian "return" since the ironic dialogue is a comic version of the dualism so stridently insisted on in "Higher Laws." The function of the irony of self-disparagement here and elsewhere is to relax the tensions of the earlier chapter and enable the reader to return, chastened and invigorated but not left in the air of the inhuman abstraction of an impossible dualism.

It is of some interest that these two patterned side trips off the main itinerary of *Walden* cannot be discovered in the first prospectus, the earliest version of the book as reconstructed by J. Lyndon Shanley.[6] That first version lacks also "Conclusion" and thus lacks the ultimate return from Walden with its poignant admission: "I do not say that John or Jonathan will realize all this." In fact, almost none of the specimen passages cited above appear in the "first" *Walden*. Their absence suggests that whatever else Thoreau did with his masterpiece between 1847 and 1854, he discovered the possibilities of a pulsating, dynamic style which would engage the reader, secure his willing suspension of inertia, and involve him in a series of literary journeys seemingly of the greatest import, but not journeys without end.

In style as well as structure, in language as well as idea, then, Thoreau recapitulates the archetypal Romantic theme of rebirth. His significant contribution to the theme is his recognition that the moment of spiritual rebirth is not infinite, that the walk cannot be prolonged indefinitely, that return is inevitable. To death and rebirth, he adds re-entry. In a way, readers of Thoreau have always sensed this characteristic, seeking, however, to define it in philosophical or ethical terms, "the poet-naturalist," for example. But Thoreau, we must remember, is a literary artist, whose service to philosophy and ethics is to provide a fresh literary experience of perhaps old ideas and values. At its best his writing renews the vitality of a life of principle by providing the reader vicarious participation in a compelling version. His rhetorically extreme and seemingly intransigent claims for such a life, however, carry their own ironic qualification and thus make it available as ideal reality, if not as normal actuality.

Thoreau the man had his forbidding rigidities and intransigencies, of course, and Thoreau the almost priggish letter-writer even more. Such static intransigency does pop up now and then

---

[6] *The Making of Walden* (Chicago, 1957).

in the writing on "simplicity" or "Higher Laws" and occasionally threatens to dominate an entire work, "Life Without Principle," but only rarely. More often the wit, the humor, the irony render Romantic idealism accessible as a guide to life at its best rather than a monstrous abstraction existentially, perhaps, worthless.

The companions of Henry Thoreau's literary walks achieve a concrete experience of Romantic idealism, perhaps ultimately inaccessible in any other way. The dynamism of Thoreau's best writing takes us momentarily out of ourselves to that heaven-approaching plane from which the world of normality is seen and judged. We are reluctant to depart and, once there, perhaps more reluctant to return. The movement of Thoreau's prose enables us to do both and thus extract the maximum benefit from both the going and the coming back.

Joseph J. Moldenhauer

Paradox in *Walden*

I fear chiefly lest my expression may not be extra-vagant *enough, may not wander far enough beyond the narrow limits of my daily experience, so as to be adequate to the truth of which I have been convinced.* Extra-vagance! *it depends on how you are yarded. . . . I desire to speak somewhere* without *bounds; like a man in a waking moment, to men in their waking moments; for I am convinced that I cannot exaggerate enough even to lay the foundation of a true expression.*[1]

I

The idiosyncrasies of Thoreau's personality and opinions are so absorbing that "paradox" has always been a key term in Thoreau

Reprinted from *Twentieth Century Interpretations of Walden,* ed. Richard Ruland (Englewood Cliffs, N.J.: Prentice-Hall, Inc., 1968), pp. 73–84, a revised text with the present title, by permission of *The Graduate Journal.* Originally published as "The Extra-vagant Maneuver: Paradox in *Walden,*" *The Graduate Journal,* VI (Winter 1964), 132–46. Copyright © 1964 by The Board of Regents of The University of Texas.
[1] *The Writings of Henry David Thoreau,* Walden Edition, 20 vols. (Boston, 1906), II (*Walden*), 357.

scholarship. Critic of government and relentless reporter of tortoises, Platonic dreamer and statistician of tree rings, Transcendental friend who calls for "pure hate" to underprop his love,[2] Thoreau invites description as paradoxical, enigmatic, or even perverse. But as Joseph Wood Krutch maintains, "to unite without incongruity things ordinarily thought of as incongruous *is* the phenomenon called Thoreau."[3] In *Walden* this propensity toward the resolved contradiction may be observed in full flower. Here Thoreau talks only of himself, yet "brag[s] for humanity." Self-isolated in a spot as remote, he says, as Cassiopeia's Chair, he strolls to the village "every day or two." Renouncing materialism for a poetic and mystic life, he proudly reports his own prudential efficiency, and documents his "economic" success with balance sheets. Bewailing the limitations of science, he painstakingly measures the depth of the pond and counts the bubbles in its ice.

The dominant stylistic feature of *Walden* is paradox—paradox in such quantity and of such significance that we are reminded of the works of Donne, Sir Thomas Browne, and other English metaphysical writers. Thoreau's paradoxical assertion—for instance, "Much is published, but little printed"—seems self-contradictory and opposed to reason. As a poetic device it has intimate connections with metaphor, because it remains an absurdity only so long as we take the terms exclusively in their conventional discursive senses. The stumbling block disappears when we realize that Thoreau has shifted a meaning, has constructed a trope or a play on words. The pun, that highly compressed form of comparison in which two or more logically disparate meanings are forced to share the same phonemic unit, lends itself admirably to Thoreau's purpose and underlies many of his paradoxes, including the example cited above. The peculiar impact of the paradox lies in our recognition that an expected meaning has been dislocated by another, remaining within our field of vision but somewhat out of focus. We are given, in Kenneth Burke's splendid phrase, a "perspective by incongruity."

The user of paradox thus defines or declares by indirection, frustrating "rational" expectations about language. Shortly before the publication of *Walden*, another New England Transcendentalist, the theologian Horace Bushnell, affirmed the usefulness of the

---

[2] *Ibid.,* I, 305. See Perry Miller, *Consciousness in Concord* (Boston, 1958), pp. 80–103, for a full examination of the paradoxes in Transcendental friendship.

[3] Joseph Wood Krutch, *Henry David Thoreau* (New York, 1948), p. 286.

device, declaring that "we never come so near to a truly well rounded view of any truth, as when it is offered paradoxically; that is, under contradictions; that is, when under two or more dictions, which, when taken as dictions, are contrary to one another." [4] In *Walden*, Thoreau wants to convey truths of the most unconventional sort—to bring other minds into proximity and agreement with his own attitudes and beliefs. He employs paradox not only for its galvanic effect in persuasion (i.e., as a verbal shock-treatment which reorients the audience), but for the special precision of statement it affords.

At the outset of Thoreau's literary career, his friend Emerson criticized the *"mannerism"* of "A Winter Walk," objecting most strenuously to the oxymorons: "for example, to call a cold place sultry, a solitude public, a wilderness *domestic....*" [5] And we are not astonished to find that Thoreau himself deprecated the very instrument he used so skillfully. When he set down in the *Journal* a list of his "faults," the first item was "Paradoxes,—saying just the opposite,—a style which may be imitated." [6] On another occasion he complained that a companion, probably Ellery Channing, "tempts me to certain licenses of speech.... He asks for a paradox, an eccentric statement, and too often I give it to him." [7] But in spite of these warnings and hesitations (which, incidentally, are echoed in the reservations of some of his most sympathetic later critics), Thoreau did not abandon the paradoxical style. Richard Whately, the author of his college rhetoric text, had acknowledged, though rather reluctantly, the value of the device in argumentation. Thoreau's seventeenth-century reading illustrated its rich literary possibilities. Most important, his ironic sensibility embraced paradox. Thoreau wisely followed what he called the crooked bent of his genius and practiced a rhetoric appropriate to his aims.

These aims were in part determined by the character of Transcendental thinking, with its emphasis upon the perception of a spiritual reality behind the surfaces of things. Nature for the Transcendentalist was an expression of the divine mind; its phenomena, when rightly seen, revealed moral truths. By means of proper perception, said Emerson, "man has access to the entire

---

[4] Horace Bushnell, *God in Christ: Three Discourses ... with a Preliminary Dissertation on Language* (Hartford, 1849), p. 55; cited in Charles Feidelson, Jr., *Symbolism and American Literature* (Chicago, 1953), p. 156.
[5] Walter Harding and Carl Bode, eds., *The Correspondence of Henry David Thoreau* (New York, 1958), p. 137: RWE to HDT, Sept. 18, 1843.
[6] Thoreau, XIII, 7, n.
[7] *Ibid.*, XII, 165.

mind of the Creator," and "is himself the creator" of his own world.[8] The pure, healthy, and self-reliant man, whose mind is in harmony with the Over-Soul, continually discerns the miraculous in the common. But for the timid or degraded man, whose eyes are clouded by convention, nature will appear a "ruin or . . . blank." Idealism is the Transcendentalist's necessary premise: it assures him that things conform to thoughts. By way of demonstration, Emerson tells his uninitiated reader to look through his legs at an inverted landscape. Thoreau was sufficiently tough-minded, and sufficiently interested in the details of natural phenomena, to resist the systematic translation of nature into ideas and moral precepts which Emersonian theory implied. He placed as much emphasis upon the "shams and delusions" which hinder men from "seeing" nature as upon the spiritual meanings of individual natural objects. But he always believed that to recognize one's relations with nature is the basis of moral insight; and he was convinced that the obstacles to this wisdom were removed by the simplification of life. Strip away the artificial, Thoreau tells the "desperate" man, and you will be able to read nature's language. Reality, the "secret of things," lurks under appearances, waiting to be seen. Describing his conversations with the French-Canadian woodchopper, Thoreau says he tried to "maneuver" him "to take the spiritual view of things." [9]

The language of *Walden* is, in a very immediate sense, strategic. The problem Thoreau faced there—and to some extent in all his writings—was to create in his audience the "waking moments" in which they could appreciate "the truth of which [he had] been convinced." In other words, he tries to wrench into line with his own the reader's attitudes toward the self, toward society, toward nature, and toward God. He "translates" the reader, raising him out of his conventional frame of reference into a higher one, in which extreme truths become intelligible. To these ends Thoreau employs a rhetoric of powerful exaggeration, antithesis, and incongruity. Habitually aware of the "common sense," the dulled perception that desperate life produces, he could turn the world of his audience upside-down by rhetorical means. He explores new resources of meaning in their "rotten diction" and challenges ingrained habits of thought and action with ennobling alternatives: "Read not the Times," he exhorts in "Life Without Principle."

---

[8] *The Complete Works of Ralph Waldo Emerson,* Centenary Edition, 12 vols. (Boston, 1903), I, 64.
[9] Thoreau, II, 166.

"Read the Eternities." [10] With all the features of his characteristic extravagance—hyperbole, wordplay, paradox, mock-heroics, loaded questions, and the ironic manipulation of cliché, proverb, and allusion—Thoreau urges new perspectives upon his reader. These rhetorical distortions or dislocations, rather than Transcendental doctrines *per se*, are Thoreau's means of waking his neighbors up. They exasperate, provoke, tease, and cajole; they are the chanticleer's call to intellectual morning; they make *Walden*, in the words of John Burroughs, "the most delicious piece of brag in literature." [11]

II

Walden is not, of course, merely a sophisticated sermon. It is the story of an experiment; a narrative; a fable. In 1851, with his "life in the woods" four years behind him and the book which would celebrate that experience, which would give it a permanent artistic and moral focus, still far from finished, Thoreau wrote, "My facts shall be falsehoods to the common sense. I would so state facts that they shall be significant, shall be myths or mythologic." [12] Even the most hortatory sections of the book are grounded in this "mythology" or significant fiction. I hope to demonstrate that paradox is apposite to the literary design of *Walden:* its themes, symbols, characters, and plot.

As a number of literary theorists have maintained, we can to some extent isolate "a fictional hero with a fictional audience" in any literary work.[13] The "I" of *Walden*, Thoreau as its narrator and hero, is a deliberately created verbal personality. This dramatized Thoreau should not be confused in critical analysis with the surveyor and pencil-maker of Concord: the *persona* stands in the same relation to the man as *Walden*—the symbolic gesture, the imaginative re-creation—stands to the literal fact of the Walden adventure. The narrator is a man of various moods and rhetorical stances, among them the severe moralist, the genial companion, the bemused "hermit," and the whimsical trickster who regards his

---

[10] *Ibid.,* IV, 475.

[11] Burroughs, "Henry D. Thoreau," *Indoor Studies* (Boston, 1895), p. 29.

[12] Thoreau, IX, 99.

[13] Northrop Frye, *Anatomy of Criticism* (Princeton, 1957), p. 53. See also W. K. Wimsatt, Jr., *The Verbal Icon* (Lexington, Ky., 1954), p. xv; John Crowe Ransom, *The World's Body* (New York, 1938), p. 247ff; René Wellek, "Closing Statement," *Style in Language,* ed. Thomas A. Sebeok (New York, 1960), p. 414.

experiment as a sly joke on solid citizens. The mellowest of all his moods is the one we find, for instance, in "Baker Farm," "Brute Neighbors," and "House-Warming," where he pokes fun at his own zeal as an idealist and reformer. In all his roles he conveys a sense of his uniqueness, the separateness of his vision from that of his townsmen.

The "fictional audience" of *Walden* likewise requires our attention. In defining it I take a hint from Burke, who in "Antony in Behalf of the Play" distinguishes between the play-mob and the spectator-mob as audiences for the oration in *Julius Caesar*. The reader of *Walden*, like Shakespeare's spectator, adopts a double perspective, weighing the speaker's statements both in terms of the fictional circumstance and in terms of their relevance to his own experience. I would distinguish a range of response *within* the dramatic context of *Walden* from an external or critical response. The reader in part projects himself into the role of a hypothetical "listener," whom the narrator addresses directly; and in part he stands at a remove, overhearing this address. Psychologically, we are "beside ourselves in a sane sense," [14] both spectators who respond to *Walden* as an aesthetic entity and vicarious participants in the verbal action. As spectators, or what I will call "readers," we are sympathetic toward the witty and engaging narrator. As projected participants, or what I will term "audience," we must imagine ourselves committed to the prejudices and shortsightedness which the narrator reproves, and subject to the full tone of the address.

The rhetoric of Walden, reflecting in some measure the lecture origins of the early drafts, assumes an initially hostile audience. Thoreau sets up this role for us by characterizing, in the first third of "Economy," a mixed group of silent listeners who are suspicious of the speaking voice. He would address "poor students," "the mass of men who are discontented," and "that seemingly wealthy, but most terribly impoverished class of all, who have accumulated dross." In addition Thoreau creates individual characters who express attitudes to be refuted by the narrator, and who serve as foils for his wit. These are stylized figures, briefly but deftly sketched, who heckle or complain or interrogate. Their function is overtly to articulate the implicit doubts of the audience. "A certain class of unbelievers," "some inveterate cavillers," "housewives . . . and elderly people," "my tailoress," "the hard-featured farmer,"

---

[14] Thoreau, II, 149.

"a factory-owner"—such lightly delineated types register their protests against Thoreau's farming techniques, his lack of charity, his conclusions about the pond's depth, his manner of making bread, and even the cleanliness of his bed linen. Their objections tend to be "impertinent," despite Thoreau's disclaimer early in "Economy," to the lower as well as the higher aspects of the experiment. He answers these animadversions with every form of wit: puns, irony, redefinition, paradoxes, twisted proverbs, overstatements, Biblical allusions (cited by a "heathen" to shame the Christian audience), and gymnastic leaps between the figurative and the literal. It is in this context of debate, of challenge and rejoinder, of provocation and rebuttal and exhortation, that the language of *Walden* must be understood. Thoreau's rhetoric is a direct consequence of the way he locates himself as narrator with respect to a hostile fictional audience. The dramatic status of the speaker and his hearers accounts for the extraordinary "audibility" of *Walden* as well as for the aesthetic distance between author and reader.

Our bifurcation into spectator and participant is most intense in the hortatory and satirical passages. In the latter role, we are incredulous, shocked, and subject to the direct persuasive techniques of the argument. As spectator, on the other hand, we applaud Thoreau's rhetorical devastation of the premises of his fictional audience, and, if we find the instructive and polemical statements in *Walden* meaningful, as we most certainly can, we recognize that they are contained by the literary structure, and that they must, as statements about life, be understood first within that context. Even the reader who conforms to the type of the fictional audience, and who brings to *Walden* a full-blown set of prejudices against Thoreauvian "economy," does not stay long to quarrel with the narrator. The force of Thoreau's ridicule encourages him to quit the stage. For the participant, *Walden* is "an invitation to life's dance"; [15] the sympathetic reader dances with Thoreau from the start.

Thoreau's paradoxes are also congenial to the "comic" themes and narrative movement of *Walden*. Using the distinctions of Northrop Frye, we can consider comedy one of the four "mythoi" or recurrent patterns of plot development which may appear in any genre. The "mythos of spring" or comic plot is typified by a rising movement, "from a society controlled by habit, ritual bondage,

---

[15] E. B. White, "Walden—1954," *Yale Review,* XLIV (1954), 13. White does not distinguish between reader and fictional audience.

arbitrary law and the older characters to a society controlled by youth and pragmatic freedom ... a movement from illusion to reality." [16] Frye's generalization may call to mind a passage in "Conclusion" where Thoreau proclaims the joys of the "awakened" man: "new, universal, and more liberal laws will begin to establish themselves around and within him; or the old laws be expanded, and interpreted in his favor in a more liberal sense, and he will live with the license of a higher order of beings." On the human level, *Walden*'s narrator performs this ascent. On the level of nature, the green life of spring and summer must rise from old winter's bondage, repeating the hero's own movement and prefiguring the spiritual transformation of his audience, "man in the larva state."

Following a traditional comic pattern, Thoreau represents in *Walden* two worlds: the narrator's private paradise and the social wasteland he has abandoned. Each of these polar worlds has its basic character type and body of symbols. The narrator is the *Eiron,* the virtuous or witty character whose actions are directed toward the establishment of an ideal order. The audience and hecklers, who take for granted "what are deemed 'the most sacred laws of society,' " [17] serve as the *Alazon* or impostor. This comic type is a braggart, misanthrope, or other mean-spirited figure, usually an older man, who resists the hero's efforts to establish harmony but who is often welcomed into the ideal order when the hero succeeds. The narrator of *Walden*, both clever and good, withdraws from a society of "skin-flint[s]" to a greenwood world at the pond. His pastoral sanctuary is represented in images of moisture, freedom, health, the waking state, fertility, and birth. The society he leaves behind is described in images of dust, imprisonment, disease, blindness, lethargy, and death. Upon these symbolic materials Thoreau builds many of his paradoxes. In his verbal attacks upon the old society, whose "idle and musty virtues" he finds as ridiculous as its vices, the narrator assumes a satirical or denunciatory pose. When he records his simple *vita nuova*, that is, in the idyllic passages, his tone becomes meditative or ecstatic.

III

But it is, after all, to the dusty world or wasteland that *Walden*'s fictional audience belongs. Despite their dissatisfactions, they are

---

[16] Frye, p. 169.
[17] Thoreau, II, 355.

committed to this life and its values, and blind to the practical as well as the spiritual advantages of the experiment. The narrator, far from being a misanthropic skulker, wishes to communicate his experience of a more harmonious and noble life. His language serves this end: the first rhetorical function of paradox is to make the audience entertain a crucial doubt. Do they value houses? Thoreau calls them prisons, almshouses, coffins, and family tombs. Farming? It is digging one's own grave. Equipment and livestock? Herds are the keepers of men, not men of herds; and men are "the tools of their tools." Traditional knowledge and a Harvard education? Thoreau describes them as impediments to wisdom. Financial security, or "something [laid up] against a sick day," is the cause of sickness in the man who works for it. Fine and fashionable clothing is a form of decoration more barbaric than tattooing, which is only "skin-deep." The landlord's sumptuous furnishings are really "traps" (an elaborate pun) which hold the holder captive. The railroad, marvel of the industrial age, is a means of transportation ultimately slower than going afoot. Religion, Thoreau tells his pious audience, is a "cursing of God" and distrust of themselves. "Good business," the bulwark of their culture, is the quickest way to the devil. In short, says Thoreau, "the greater part of what my neighbors call good I believe in my soul to be bad, and if I repent of anything, it is very likely to be my good behavior. What demon possessed me that I behaved so well?" These paradoxes, often executed with brilliant humor, jostle and tumble the listener's perspective. To be sure, the narrator is a self-acknowledged eccentric —but he is not a lunatic. Thoreau makes sense in his own terms, and the fictional audience no longer can in theirs.

At the same time as he makes nonsense of the audience's vocabulary with satirical paradoxes, Thoreau appropriates some of its key terms to describe the special values of his life in the woods. For example, though he despises commerce he would conduct a profitable "trade" with the "Celestial Empire." In this second body of rhetorical devices Thoreau again exploits polarities of symbol and idea, and not without irony. But these paradoxes differ sharply in their function from the satirical ones. They attach to the hero's world, to nature and simplified action, the deep connotations of worth which social involvements and material comforts evoke for the desperate man. Thoreau astounds and disarms the audience when he calls his experiment a "business" and renders his accounts to the half- and quarter-penny. By means of this appropriately inappropriate language he announces the incompatibility of his livelihood and his neighbor's, and simultaneously suggests interesting resemblances. Thoreau's enterprise, like the businessman's, requires risks, demands perseverance, and holds out the lure of rewards. The statistical passages of "Economy" and "The Bean-Field" are equivocal. On the one hand, they prove the narrator's ability to beat the thrifty Yankee at his own game; on the other, they parody the Yankee's obsession with finance. Thoreau's argument that a man achieves success in proportion as he reduces his worldly needs is likewise paradoxical, a queer analogue to the commercial theory of increasing profits by lowering costs. He reinforces this unconventional economic principle by declaring that the simple life is to be carefully cultivated and jealously preserved: "Give me the poverty that enjoys true wealth." Similarly he contrasts the rich harvest which a poet reaps from a farm with the *relatively* worthless cash crop, and is eager to acquire the Hollowell place before its owner destroys it with "improvements." I would also include in this category of paradoxes Thoreau's constant reference to fish, berries, and other common natural objects in the language of coins, precious gems, and rare metals; his praise of the humble simpleton as an exalted sage; his assertion that the woods and ponds are religious sanctuaries; and his description of his labors as pastimes and his solitude as companionable. Some related statements carry the mystical overtones of the New Testament: "Not till we are lost, in other words, not till we have lost the world, do we begin to find ourselves." "Walden was dead and is alive again." All these apparent contradictions support Thoreau's triumphant subjectivism in *Walden*, his running proclamation that "The universe constantly and obediently answers to our conceptions." [18] The highest and most sincere conception yields the noblest life.

By nature a dialectical instrument, the paradox is thus stylistically integral to this severely dialectical work. Viewed generally, the two large groups of paradoxes reflect the comic structure of *Walden* and its two major themes: the futility of the desperate life and the rewards of enlightened simplicity. With the paradoxes of the first or satirical group, Thoreau declares that his listener's goods are evils, his freedom slavery, and his life a death. Those of the second group, corresponding rhetorically to the recurrent symbolism of metamorphosis, affirm that the values of the natural and Transcendental life arise from what the audience would deprecate as valueless. In these paradoxes, the beautiful is contained in the

---

[18] *Ibid.*, II, 108.

ugly, the truly precious in the seemingly trivial, and the springs of life in the apparently dead.

As *Walden* progresses the proportion of the first to the second kind gradually changes. The rhetoric of the early chapters is very largely one of trenchant denunciation, directed against the desperate life. That of the later chapters is predominantly serene, playful, and rapturous. Thoreau creates the impression of a growing concord between himself and his audience by allowing the caustic ironies and repudiations of "Economy" to shift by degrees to the affirmations of "Spring" and "Conclusion." Thoreau the outsider becomes Thoreau the magnanimous insider, around whom reasonable men and those who love life may gather. Rhetorically and thematically, as the book proceeds, the attack becomes the dance. . . .

Charles R. Anderson

The Leap

"To travel and 'descry new lands' is to think new thoughts, and have new imaginings," he had written in his *Journal* a decade before: "The deepest and most original thinker is the farthest travelled." (LJ, 153) [1] This is what is meant, on the second and more significant level, by his whimsical remark: "I have travelled a good deal in Concord." Throughout *Walden*, local images are extended to global ones by imaginary travel. As he looks across the pond from his cabin door, "the opposite shore . . . stretched away toward the prairies of the West and the steppes of Tartary."

From *The Magic Circle of Walden* by Charles R. Anderson (New York: Holt, Rinehart and Winston, Inc., 1968), pp. 268–78. Copyright © 1968 by Charles R. Anderson. Reprinted by permission of Holt, Rinehart and Winston, Inc.

[1] [Parenthetical page numbers preceded by "LJ" refer to Thoreau's "Lost Journal" (Perry Miller, *Consciousness in Concord,* 1958); those preceded by "J" and a Roman numeral refer to the *Journal,* vols. 7–20 of the 1906 *Writings of Henry David Thoreau* but numbered separately I–XIV; those preceded by neither letters nor Roman numerals refer to *Walden,* vol. 2 in the 1906 *Writings.* Abbreviated titles in several footnotes have been expanded by the compiler.]

(97) When the ice is cut in winter to be shipped to Asia by Yankee clipper, as has been pointed out, the pure Walden water is mingled with the sacred water of the Ganges. This is not cartographic window dressing. Instead, these are gleanings from his great storehouse of reading in Western and Oriental travel books; more importantly, they are allusions to the culture of American Indians and East Indians that he studied so intensively. Concord township is linked, by thought and imagination, to the lands and literatures of the world.

The final chapter of *Walden* contains the greatest concentration of travels, travelers, and foreign parts to be found in any one place in all Thoreau's writings. But the facts here, as always, are only starting points for figures of speech. There are two kinds of travel images, linear and circular. The latter carry only negative meanings. Brief mention is made of the migrations of the goose and bison, each of whom "keeps pace with the seasons," only to remind us of the annual cycle he is still trying to escape from. Globetrotting is lightly disparaged as an exercise in futility, actually going in circles. Who wants to rush off to South Africa "to chase the giraffe," to go on expeditions to the North Pole or the sources of the Nile, to search out "a Northwest Passage around this continent"? He dismisses the whole business by saying, "It is not worth the while to go round the world to count the cats in Zanzibar," pointing his satire by reference to an actual triviality he had picked up from a recent travel book.[2] A final circular image of travel is especially interesting because of its ambiguity. In the context of globe-trotting, and so presumably with disparagement, he says: "Our voyaging is only great-circle sailing." (352) This is the navigator's term for sailing along any of the "great circles" like the equator, such a course being the shortest between any two points on the earth's surface. That is, it fits the definition of a straight line, the illusion experienced by the voyager, but it is actually an arc of the earth's sphere, and following it, he eventually comes back to where he started from.

It is only by linear images of travel that Thoreau could annihilate space. The most soaring one in *Walden* over-leaps all boundaries and leaves the planet. But first a *Journal* entry for 1851 that offers a substantial launching pad for his space flight: "We

---

[2] (354, 352–353) Walter Harding, *The Variorum Walden* (1963), 317, n. 14, identifies the book that contained such a report as Charles Pickering's *The Races of Man* (London, 1851). Thoreau read it in 1853 (*see* J, V, 392).

experience pleasure when an elevated field or even road in which we may be walking holds its level toward the horizon at a tangent to the earth, is not convex with the earth's surface, but an absolute level." (J, II, 422) Although Thoreau was well aware of the optical illusion involved in the actual phenomenon, he did not hesitate to use it metaphorically in his book. There, in "Conclusion," it becomes his greatest leap of the spirit:

> Start now on that farthest western way, which does not pause at the Mississippi or the Pacific, nor conduct toward a wornout China or Japan, but leads on direct, a tangent to this sphere, summer and winter, day and night, sun down, moon down, and at last earth down too. (354–355)

There is an even more extravagant flight in an early *Journal* passage, too fanciful to have been included in *Walden* but deserving quotation here because it links a linear travel image of migrating birds with the rebirth imagery in "Spring":

> To-day I feel the migratory instinct strong in me, and all my members and humors anticipate the breaking up of winter. If I yielded to this impulse, it would surely guide me to summer haunts. This indefinite restlessness and fluttering on the perch do, no doubt, prophesy the final migration of souls out of nature to a serene summer, in long harrows and waving lines in the spring weather, over what fair uplands and fertile Elysian meadows winging their way at evening and seeking a resting-place with loud cackling and uproar! (J, I, 176)

This is indeed an unusable flight of fancy, whether for bird or man, here merged into one as a symbol of the soul in its final transmigration to eternal summer.

Thoreau's other linear travel image is entirely valid, not an escape into outer space but a journey downward into the Self. The original *Journal* draft for the opening page of "Conclusion," rich in its references to external travel, ends with an alternative recommendation: "Let us migrate interiorly without intermission." (J, I, 131) In *Walden* this is expanded into a two-page conceit for internal travel. It is "validated," appropriately, by citation of two metaphysical authors, a minor poet and a master of prose. Thoreau launches his journey with a quotation from William Habington's poetic epistle to a friend, though without naming author or title:

Direct your eye right inward, and you'll find
A thousand regions in your mind
Yet undiscovered. Travel them, and be
Expert in home-cosmography.[3]

This is followed by several questions posing the alternatives of external and internal travel: "What does Africa,—what does the West stand for? Is not our own interior white on the chart? [That is, unexplored.] ... Is it the source of the Nile, or the Niger, or the Mississippi, or a Northwest Passage around this continent, that we would find?" (353) At this point the second and most important allusion comes into play. It is much more subtle, being merely the ingestion of an idea from Sir Thomas Browne's *Religio Medici*, without quotation or any direct clue to the source. About the year 1840, Thoreau had copied down in his commonplace book a passage in which Browne says he can match all that the Nile and the North Pole have to offer, "in the cosmography of myself," without the bother of travel: "We carry with us the wonders we seek without us. There is all Africa and her prodigies in us." [4]

Just how completely Thoreau assimilated this idea is shown by the answer he gives in *Walden* to his own rhetorical questions, quoted above: "Be rather the Mungo Park, the Lewis and Clark and Frobisher, of your own streams and oceans; explore your own higher latitudes. ... Nay, be a Columbus to whole new continents and worlds within you, opening new channels, not of trade, but of thought." (353) Again, this is not name-dropping but a pertinent reference to the authors of travel books he was intimately acquainted with—accounts of exploring expeditions to the heart of Africa, the American West, and a possible route around America to Cathay—topped with a salute to the symbolic explorer of new worlds. "If you would travel farther than all travellers," he concludes—"Explore thyself." (354) So he gives new life to an old cliché.

His final linear image of travel annihilates all space by drawing it into himself, making it an idea in the mind and a metaphor on the page. "As travellers go round the world and report natural

---

[3] (353) Walter Harding, *The Variorum Walden* (1963), 316, note 4, points out a slip in the first line: "eye right" instead of "eye-sight."

[4] K. W. Cameron, ed., *The Transcendentalists and Minerva* (1958), I, 282, prints Thoreau's extracts from Browne's *Miscellaneous Works* (Cambridge, 1831), 31—including the one here quoted. Sherman Paul, *The Shores of America* (1958), 59, points out the analogy, though apparently unaware of the proof in Thoreau's commonplace book.

objects and phenomena," he suggests in a *Journal* entry of 1851, "so faithfully let another stay at home and report the phenomena of his own life,—catalogue stars, those thoughts whose orbits are as rarely calculated as comets. . . . A meteorological journal of the mind." (J, II, 403) This is a perfect description of his own book, being completed at the time, with its program of the most intensive kind of living symbolized by the most extensive kind of travel. When reading Gibbon's memoirs he once commented: "To my mind he travels as far when he takes a book from the shelf, as if he went to the barrows of Asia." (LJ, 182) One might say the same thing after reading *Walden*, the unique memoir of Henry Thoreau.

The poet draws all things into himself—Space and Time, Nature and God—only so that he can give them out again recreated as metaphors. Just as Thoreau merged himself with all these by learning to orbit in their circles, so he learned to escape from all entrapments by vertical leaps into a newly identified life. There could be no happier way to conclude this reading of his "one book of poetry" than by examining several of those purely linear images that will point to some of the final meanings in *Walden*, the two most memorable ones coming in its "Conclusion."

One of the earliest in the book occurs in that often cited list of "enterprises" to which he has dedicated himself: "In any weather, at any hour of the day or night, I have been anxious to improve the nick of time, and notch it on my stick too; to stand on the meeting of two eternities, the past and future, which is precisely the present moment; to toe that line." (18) This is his witty version of the transcendental formula for escaping from the wheel of time by living in the Eternal Now. Again, in the same introductory chapter, "Economy," noting that the seed sends its radicle downward so that it can send its shoot upward with equal confidence, he invokes another transcendental doctrine: "Why has man rooted himself thus firmly in the earth, but that he may rise in the same proportion into the heavens above." (17) The same moral analogy is made in the next to last chapter, drawn from the new grass that shoots up in "Spring": "So our human life but dies down to its root, and still puts forth its green blade to eternity." (343) Thoreau is not often so solemnly didactic, but he found it hard to dodge the idea of Correspondence when looking for intimations of immortality.

Much more in keeping with the style of *Walden* at its best is a vignette in his central chapter "The Ponds." He begins by telling

how sometimes, returning late from the village, "partly with a view
to the next day's dinner, [I] spent the hours of midnight fishing
from a boat by moonlight." What follows is one of those miniature
anecdotes, moving by surprise from factual to figurative language,
that adorn his narrative and point up his meanings. In a timeless
mood he drifts about the pond until he feels a slight vibration along
the line:

> At length you slowly raise, pulling hand over hand, some horned
> pout squeaking and squirming to the upper air. It was very queer,
> especially in dark nights, when your thoughts had wandered to
> vast and cosmogonal themes in other spheres, to feel this faint jerk,
> which came to interrupt your dreams and link you to Nature again.
> It seemed as if I might next cast my line upward into the air, as
> well as downward into this element, which was scarcely more dense.
> Thus I caught two fishes as it were with one hook. (194–195)

In a much earlier chapter a similar image occurs in brief: "I
would . . . fish in the sky, whose bottom is pebbly with stars." (109)
And far along in the book, in "The Pond in Winter," when he cuts
a hole in the ice and peers down into the "quiet parlor" of the
fishes looking as serene as in summer, he creates an answering
image: "Heaven is under our feet as well as over our heads." (313)
Walden Pond, with its transparent waters and its calm reflecting
surface, was a perfect source of metaphors for the heavenward leap
that transcends the limitations of earth.

The complementary aspects of pond and sky lead to a series of
images by which he tries to probe for himself. In an early *Journal*
entry he says: "I cannot see the bottom of the sky, because I cannot see to the bottom of myself. It is the symbol of my own infin-
ity." (J, I, 150) Turning to Walden Pond, a more accessible point
for measurement, he makes it into a lens of magical powers: "It is
earth's eye; looking into which the beholder measures the depth of
his own nature." (206–207) This image-and-idea from "The Ponds"
is picked up seven chapters later in "The Pond in Winter." Many
people have tried to sound the bottom of Walden without success,
he says, "paying out the rope in the vain attempt to fathom their
truly immeasurable capacity for marvellousness." Then he adds,
with feigned condescension, "While men believe in the infinite
some ponds will be thought to be bottomless." (316) Having pretended to ally himself with science, he then spreads out his survey
of the pond over some five or six pages, with the precise detail of
a limnologist.

His conclusion sounds like that of a scientific researcher: "I . . . found, to my surprise, that the line of greatest length intersected the line of greatest breadth *exactly* at the point of greatest depth." (319, 315–320) But the use to which he puts this new fact gives the game away. "What I have observed of the pond is no less true in ethics," he says, and then proceeds to apply the "rule of the two diameters" to man for the purpose of measuring the "height or depth of his character." (321–322) The page-long *jeu d'esprit* that follows has been called by one critic "a kind of superb topographical phrenology." [5] It is actually a compounding of the device of arguing by analogy: the shape of the pond added to the shape of the human head to find correspondences in the character of the man within. Phrenology by mid-century had been recognized as only a pseudo-science, and so not taken seriously, though it continued to be useful to poets as a source of metaphor (Poe, Emerson, Whitman, to name only a few). Thoreau's conceit is clearly touched with wit. It begins: "As I was desirous to recover the long lost bottom of Walden Pond, I surveyed it carefully," and so on. (315) He found its bottom and at the same time discovered the foundation of his own faith. He differed from contemporary sounders of the pond not by being scientific while they were superstitious. It was not by failing to plumb some mystery in nature that he came to believe in the infinite but by measuring "the depth of his own nature."

In a direction opposite to this downward probing is the erection of his chimney. Of course, the chimney is a fact as well as an image, the building of it being part of the "economy" of the Walden experiment, postponed for several months after the cabin was completed since he did not need it until cold weather came. This delay throws it into the chapter called "House-Warming," and the verbal play of that title is echoed all through the passage describing its construction. He concludes with a significant metaphor. After commenting on the fact that one often sees chimneys still standing long after the houses are gone, he says: "The chimney is to some extent an independent structure, standing on the ground, and rising through the house to the heavens." (267) Part of the effectiveness here is that the chimney is by its very nature symbolic and requires little contrivance on the part of the writer to make it so. Thoreau was quick to exploit its other possibilities. "I took a poet to board for a fortnight about those times," he says. It is well known that Ellery Channing was a guest at Walden during the fall

---

[5] Paul, 344. His analysis of the passage covers three pages, 342–345.

of 1845, and presumably helped with building the chimney.[6] But
Thoreau was a poet too, as well as a mason, and once again he gives
us a figure that can be reckoned as his double. At any rate, it was
he and not Channing who wrote the poem "Smoke," that concludes
his chapter and his metaphor:

> Light-winged Smoke, Icarian bird,
> Melting thy pinions in thy upward flight,
> Lark without song, and messenger of dawn,
> Circling above the hamlets as thy nest;
> Or else, departing dream, and shadowy form
> Of midnight vision, gathering up thy skirts;
> By night star-veiling, and by day
> Darkening the light and blotting out the sun;
> Go thou my incense upward from this hearth,
> And ask the gods to pardon this clear flame. (279)

Of the many poems written by Thoreau, in the conventional
sense of verse-poems, this is one of the very few that is successful
—possibly because it rises directly out of the text of *Walden*, his
one really great "poem." The sentence that launches it is part of
its meaning: "When the villagers were lighting their fires beyond
the horizon, I too gave notice to the various wild inhabitants of
Walden vale, by a smoky streamer from my chimney, that I was
awake." The woodland solitude makes an appropriate setting for
his morning ritual of kindling a fire, his ever-fresh renewal of purpose; "awake" is his constant term for being alive, the "dead"
being those who are always asleep. The sentence that follows (previously quoted in another context) is also a gloss on the poem:
"It was I and Fire that lived there." "Fire" is another double for
the narrator, also a double symbol, as has been shown: the vital
heat for sustaining life through the winter and the "flame" of his
thought or inner self. Its use in the poem proves this.

If the chimney is only indirectly a symbol for Thoreau, the
smoke is made directly so: "Go thou *my incense* upward from this
hearth." Not quite his prayer, but his fragrant burnt offering that
might stand for it, and offered quite safely in a Christian land to
the plural "gods," without specifying which ones. But why does
he ask the gods "to *pardon* this clear flame"? The last line is the
crux of the poem, and one must circle back to the first to clarify its
meaning by asking why he calls the smoke "Icarian bird"? The

---

[6] *See* Harding, *The Days of Henry Thoreau* (1965), 182.

allusion brings in the legend of Icarus, the arrogant demi-god who defied the laws of nature and hence the gods by trying to fly on man-made wings, came too near heaven and, burned by the sun's heat, fell to his death in the sea. Thoreau's smoke in its "upward flight" like a bird also challenges heaven and might seem to risk a similar fate—except that it is quickly transformed through a series of images into a lark, dawn's messenger, a dream, a vision. Still the "clear flame" of his spirit burns so brightly that its smoke "blots out the sun," and it needs a plea for pardon to keep him from verging on hubris.[7] It is almost like a prayer from one god to another, from an earthly Apollo to the heavenly one.

If Thoreau could hint at his own divinity by identifying with Apollo from time to time, he could also suggest that he has already achieved immortality. He does so by fashioning a legend of the artist of Kouroo that is a parable of his own life and vocation. It sounds like a Hindu myth, but no one has been able to discover a source for it. Happily it must be taken as an original creation, but rendered so perfectly in the guise of an Oriental scripture as to be mistaken for one. All that came directly from his reading is that Kouroo (Kooroo, Kuru) is mentioned in the *Mahabharata* and in the *Bhagvat-Geeta* as a sacred land or nation, and is referred to in the *Laws of Menu* as the country of Brahmanical sages. When Thoreau published his extracts from the last named in the *Dial* for January 1843, he included that reference and, significantly, cited Menu's dictum: "The hand of an artist employed in his art is always pure." [8] All the rest of this legend is Thoreau's own, his most impressive leap of the imagination. It begins:

> There was an artist in the city of Kouroo who was disposed to strive after perfection. One day it came into his mind to make a staff. Having considered that in an imperfect work time is an ingredient, but into a perfect work time does not enter, he said to himself, It shall be perfect in all respects, though I should do nothing else in my life. . . . His singleness of purpose and resolution, and his elevated piety, endowed him, without his knowledge, with perennial youth. As he made no compromise with Time, Time kept out of his way. (359)

By the time this artist had found a stick suitable for carving, his friends had deserted him, or died, and the city itself was a hoary

---

[7] This last point is made by F. O. Matthiessen in *American Renaissance* (1941), 166.

[8] These details are summed up by Paul, 353 note.

ruin. Before he had given it proper shape, the dynasty of the Can-
dahars was over, and with the point of his stick he wrote the name
of the last of them in the sand. Before he had polished and adorned
it, Brahma had slept and waked many times:

> But why do I stay to mention these things? When the finishing
> stroke was put to his work, it suddenly expanded before the eyes
> of the astonished artist into the fairest of all the creations of
> Brahma. He had made a new system in making a staff, a world
> with full and fair proportions.... And now he saw by the heap of
> shavings still fresh at his feet, that, for him and his work, the
> former lapse of time had been an illusion.... The material was
> pure, and his art was pure; how could the result be other than
> wonderful? (360)

A final clue identifying the artist of Kouroo as Thoreau, if any
were needed, can be found in his letter to a friend, in the context
of his own life and work and with a reference to Brahmans: "How
admirably the artist is made to accomplish his self-culture by devotion to his art!" [9] The letter was written in December 1853, about
the same time the legend was being added to the book. It is clearly
a parable of Thoreau's own labors to create a perfect work of art
in *Walden*, polishing and revising it through eight separate drafts
over a period of as many years—all but literally devoting his
life to it. His dedication and singleness of purpose endowed him
also "with perennial youth." As the carver of Kouroo aspired
upward, fashioning his simple staff, as the original Creator of the
pond rounded it with his hand into an object of natural beauty and
symbolic significance, so Thoreau shaped his own experience into
the magic circle of *Walden*—and then made his leap out of it by
translating his facts from earth to heaven. If man is to escape from
the trap of time and the limitations of nature, according to this
book, he will be able to do so only through the immortality of art.

---

[9] *See* Thoreau's *Correspondence* (1958), 311 (letter to H. G. O. Blake).